BOB MATHIAS
Champion of Champions

BOB MATHIAS
Champion of Champions

by
JIM SCOTT

PRENTICE-HALL, INC.
NEW YORK

Printed in the United States of America

INTRODUCTION

by
Daniel J. Ferris

ON PAGE 242 OF THIS BOOK JIM SCOTT QUOTES ME AS saying: "Records don't lie." I was talking then about the achievements of Bob Mathias and Jim Thorpe. But that comparison is irrelevant. This book is a record of an exemplary life, one which proves the fact that America's greatest strength is in its youth.

The thing I like most about Bob Mathias is not that he has brought victory to his country through his prowess, but that he has upheld the principles of amateur athletics for all the world to see. Bob has conquered obstacles that have licked older, more experienced men, but has remained modest and unassuming. This is the essence of true sportsmanship.

I wish every youngster would read this biography and be inspired to model his own life after the splendid pattern Bob Mathias has set. I consider it a privilege to write these few words to introduce a young man who is truly a champion of champions.

Daniel J. Ferris

Secretary-Treasurer

AMATEUR ATHLETIC UNION
OF THE UNITED STATES

CONTENTS

Chapter 1

TULARE'S FIRST FAMILY

FOR TWO LONG JULY DAYS THE CITIZENS OF TULARE HAD held their breaths. In homes, stores, offices, people had broken their routines by rushing together every time a news flash came over the radio or from the *Tulare Advance-Register*. "What's it now?" they asked one another, straining to catch the latest bulletin. "Did he make it?" "Is Bob ahead?"

Sometimes the knots broke out into wild spontaneous cheering. Sometimes faces grew long, there were sighs of disappointment, lips firmed as their owners silently assured themselves that "our Bob" would still come through.

On the other side of the globe, Robert Bruce Mathias, the most famous and one of the youngest members of the snug little community nestled in the cotton fields of California's San Joaquin Valley, was battling against older, more experienced athletes from all over the world to clinch victory for his country in the 1952 Olympic Games at Helsinki. He had elected to do it in the punishing two-day, ten-event decathlon grind, most grueling test of an athlete's stamina and ability, the nearest thing to the ancient Greek games whose victorious heroes are still remembered two thousand and more years later.

The first day's tension grew as the word came that Bob's leg had been slightly injured and was obviously giving him pain. But the five events ended with him still fighting. Family, friends, strangers who knew Tulare's pride only from a worshipful distance, debated late into the night the chances for their favorite's success in the events of Saturday, July 26.

Morning found them glued to radios, as the broadcasts from Finland commenced again.

"Can he do it?" asked the nervous, more to conceal their own excitement than to express doubt. "Of course he can," came the inevitable answer. "Bob won't let us down."

Then the bulletins started coming. At first they were disheartening, and as time wore on, it almost seemed that the tall, handsome boy might not break the record he had set in the same events when he won the American Decathlon championship at Tulare. He had failed to better his previous performances in the broad jump, the hurdles and the discus. There were still the pole vault, the javelin throw and, last of all, the 1500-meter run for the boy who they knew must be dropping with tiredness.

At last a gigantic cheer went up from the stands in darkening Helsinki, and far away twelve thousand Tulareans doubled it in volume. Bob had won the javelin throw. He was in! Next he was beating his way to break

2

the tape at the end of the final event to finish almost 200 points ahead of his nearest rival. A new champion had joined the immortals of athletic history.

Sitting quietly that night with her husband, Mrs. Charles Mathias choked with tears of relief, of gratitude, of pride. Her Robert had come through again, just as he always had.

Perhaps her thoughts drifted back to a fine spring day eleven years before, and she saw again a scrawny kid following his big brother to the playground a couple of blocks from home.

The kid was ten years old and with his rumpled brown hair, his scarecrow shoulders, his faded blue jeans and his T-shirt, he looked no different from the thousands of shavers who frequent playgrounds throughout the country. His big brother, a promising athlete, was meeting the grammar school coach for private instruction in the high jump. Idolizing his brother, the kid had tagged along.

When the coach appeared he immediately got busy with the older boy. They paid no attention to the skinny youngster who dawdled dejectedly at the side of the high jump pit, idly sifting sand through his fingers. "Why don't they let me try, too," he wondered. "I bet I can do it."

But the other two continued to ignore him as they concentrated on the jumping. All went smoothly until the bar was raised to the four-foot level. Then the pupil missed. He missed again—and again. Calling a halt, the coach took his charge aside to allow him to rest and to lecture him on what he was doing wrong. While

3

they were occupied, the skinny kid thrilled to a wild impulse. "They're busy, they'll never notice," he told himself. "I'm gonna try it."

He walked around in front of the bar and studied it. He realized that if he were standing next to it, the bamboo would tuck under his chin. He whistled. "Wow! Pretty high for a first time." But he had made up his mind to try. Gathering speed, he hurled himself at the pole.

At that moment his brother and the coach looked back at the pit. Their jaws dropped as they saw the kid catapulting off the ground in a formless pinwheel of arms and legs. The coach flinched. "He's gonna get hurt!" he thought. But the straining little body sailed cleanly over the bar!

Dusting himself off, the kid noticed their looks of consternation. He reflected that he probably had been impolite, mixing in like this. He blurted out an apology. "I'm sorry. I was just foolin' around."

"Foolin' around?" echoed the coach in disbelief. "Bob, how would you like some coaching, too?"

The coach was W. J. (Bill) Walker, principal and physical education director of Wilson Grammar School, which the two boys attended. The older boy was Eugene Mathias, three years Bob's senior.

Before that year was out, Bob Mathias, under Walker's patient guidance, was to high jump four feet, eight inches, two inches higher than his head. But the even more fantastic climax to that brief schoolyard drama was not to come until seven years later when, before 70,000 madly applauding spectators in Empire

Stadium, London, Bob Mathias mounted the Olympic victory podium as the youngest performer ever to win the decathlon.

He had done it against unbelievable odds. The night before he had wound up with officials holding flashlights to illuminate the runways, and a steady rain making a gumbo of the field. He was not supposed to win it. No one in his teens ever had entered this most trying of all competitions before, let alone triumph in international company. The repetition of this 1948 victory at Helsinki four years later made him the only athlete ever to take successive decathlon titles. Experts were now willing to concede that Bob Mathias was the greatest all-around athlete of all time.

Even more wondrous than his records, however, was his ability to overcome the series of heartbreaking obstacles that made his climb to success much steeper than most. For a time a serious childhood illness threatened to cut short any of his plans for an athletic future. Many of the skills required in the decathlon he was forced to learn at very short notice. And in crucial meets he was plagued by bad weather and human mistakes.

But his crowning glory is that, for all his laurels, trophies and publicity, Bob Mathias remains the same unassuming, polite, friendly, playful, yet quietly determined lad that he was when he made that first "impossible" jump.

Against his true story there is a hollow ring to the fictional derring-do of the whole panel of boyhood heroes from Stover of Yale and Baseball Joe, Tom Swift and the Rover Boys, to Jack Armstrong and Frank Merriwell, Li'l Abner and Ozark Ike. The nation now boasts a real-life prototype of the All-American boy.

No cosmic omen burned in the heavens when Bob was born. He sprang from a background that was only a variation of the melting pot that has made America great. He is the product of a happy combination of sound upbringing, clean living, ample opportunities, and good fortune, ingredients to be found in countless American homes. But he had the resourcefulness of character and the diligence to take the fullest advantage of them.

Bob's ancestors were valiant pioneers who first dared a perilous ocean journey and then pressed onward from the crowded Eastern seaboard of America to wider horizons in the expanding West, following always the promise of a better future. His father, Dr. Charles Milfred Mathias, now one of the best-known general practitioners in California, himself had journeyed from Moulton, Iowa, where his own father, of Dutch-Irish-French extraction, had settled, to Oklahoma. There, at the University of Oklahoma, where he received his M. D., he met the blonde, petite Lillian Harris. They were married while he was still in medical school.

The two had many interests in common. Lillian was also of pioneer stock, stemming from tall forebears of German-Swedish descent. Like her husband, she was an excellent student, a hard worker, a sports-lover. Often she would travel two hundred miles to see her six-foot, blonde, blue-eyed beau change on the football field from a quiet, soft-spoken scholar to the hard charger

6

on defense, the sure blocker and pass receiver on offense who was an All-Missouri Valley choice in 1923 and 1924.

The couple's first child, Eugene, was born within a year of their marriage. The new parents reveled in their heir's every move and, having both grown up in sizable families, they promised themselves that he would not be the last.

After finishing school, Dr. Mathias, a member of the Naval Reserve, entered the service and was assigned to San Diego to intern as a Navy surgeon. Near the end of his tour of duty, while debating taking a post on Guam, he heard of a staff opening at the new County General Hospital at Tulare, a small dairy, fruit, and cotton center midway between Los Angeles and San Francisco. Before leaving the country, he decided to look the town over.

When he drove into Tulare from San Diego it was already dark. The wide, clean streets were pleasantly quiet, the lights glowed with a friendly twinkle, and the cheerful stores and sedate houses cast such a cozy, beckoning look that the doctor was instantly won over.

"This is for me!" he said to himself. Watching the citizens ambling genially about their business, sniffing the fragrant greenery girding the houses, breathing the bracing air of the California evening, he realized that the dream town he had always pictured as the ideal site to raise a family was right here before his eyes. He decided, even before he set foot in the hospital, to take the position, if he proved acceptable.

The next day when he was interviewed by hospital

7

officials he "sold" himself as easily as Tulare had conquered him. That was the beginning of a family-town love affair that was to grow until the names of the two are almost synonymous. Railroad men who pass through Tulare now call it "Mathiasville."

Mrs. Mathias already was expecting her second child when she moved into her first Tulare home, a modest house on Apricot Street. Neighbors who "howdied" the mother-to-be little realized that they were also inquiring about the health of a being who was to put the name of their small community on lips across the seven seas.

Dr. Mathias was to transmit to his famous offspring the skeleton of the rugged physique that he had in turn inherited from his father. But it was only with proper diet and conditioning and after a hard fight against childhood diseases that it was to flesh out into one of the most ideal human figures in modern times. Without his splendid body it is questionable if any amount of will to win, of which Bob Mathias has plenty, would have been enough to make him a champion at such a tender age.

From his father Bob also got another all-important characteristic, his easy-going nature. All through the lush San Joaquin Valley "Doc" Mathias is admired for the calm assurance of his bedside manners. At junctures in Bob's career, which also has included leading Stanford's football team into the Rose Bowl, he was able to conserve valuable energy for his now-famous comethroughs by completely forgetting the tension of competition.

8

But it was really his mother who taught him how to make full use of that characteristic and from her he learned to relax under the most trying circumstances. When Bob was sick as a boy, his mother invented a technique that coaxed him into the restfulness on which his recovery so largely depended. In later life, instead of worrying in difficult situations, Bob learned to go peaceably to sleep. Thus recuperated, his system was ready to respond to the most violent demands.

From his mother Bob also took his competitive ardor and the restless audacity to try his hand at a variety of callings and to master them. His makeup is such that he seems to do his best just when he is pressed the hardest.

His home town, too, filled a major role in shaping him. Few outside California had heard of it before Bob rocketed into the headlines in 1948, but Tulare and the Mathiases have reinforced each other since first they met.

"Doc" had brought scores of Tulareans into the world and ministered to hundreds more. He and his wife had been active in the social and charitable activities of the First Methodist Church and of various organizations about town. They had been good neighbors without regard for color or creed. This fundamental of American life was instilled in Bob, and in athletic competition with all races and colors he has always maintained the highest degree of sportsmanship.

The family and town had grown together. From a population of six thousand in 1930, Tulare has more than doubled in size. A family of only three when they first arrived, the Mathiases now number six. What Bob

9

returned to Tulare in fame was only the purest essence of those small-town virtues he had been borrowing from it since childhood: the uncomplicated nature, the unaffected speech, the ready friendliness, the candid manner, the personal integrity, the spirit of adventure which refuses to admit that the frontiers of human performance are closed.

Tulare has often demonstrated its appreciation for Bob with noisy celebrations, loud cheers, warm speeches and a multitude of material rewards. It has given him a visual tribute rivaling in importance the memorial to its sons who served in World War II. On U.S. Highway 99, leading into town, signs have been erected blaring: "Tulare, Home of Bob Mathias, Olympic and U.S. Decathlon Champion."

The decathlon seems to be the favorite pastime of Tulare's small fry, and when reporters drop around to interview Bob and inquire about the sport, almost anyone in the street can explain its intricate scoring and technique. Even when time has weathered the signs and the records have become hazy, it is certain that Bob's name will live. For the bright example of his character will be held up by townsfolk—and by parents throughout the country—as the best model their children can follow.

Nor is the town itself likely to outlast its fame. The ultimate in praise was voiced at the conclusion of the 1952 U.S. decathlon championships for which the host Tulareans went all-out to make their guests feel at home. As the meet progressed and it became evident that Milton Campbell, the young Negro giant from New

Jersey, was rivaling the home-town hero in social tact as well as in the point column, Tulareans began rooting for him as much as for Mathias. Said one citizen, "I'd hate to see Bob lose the crown, but I hope young Campbell gets at least a tie."

Campbell didn't equal Bob, but he finished a strong second and looms as Bob's most serious challenger in the future. When the final event was over and Campbell was escorted to the microphone by a swarm of cheering locals, he said: "I only wish the whole world were just a small town named Tulare."

Chapter 2

BOYHOOD

AT 7:30 A.M. NOVEMBER 17, 1930, DR. CHARLES Mathias had an appointment for surgery at the Tulare County Hospital. He was to assist Dr. Frank Kohn, medical director and chief surgeon at the hospital.

It was a cold foggy morning. At 6 a.m. Mrs. Mathias was awakened suddenly by sharp pains. She sat upright in bed.

Lillian Mathias started to awaken her husband, who was deep in sleep, but she withdrew her hand.

"He's had only a few hours sleep," she told herself. "On duty most of the night at the hospital, and he needs the rest. Let's wait."

By 7 o'clock the pain had become more acute and, too, it was then time for the doctor to get up anyway for his hospital date. So Mrs. Mathias touched her husband's hand and he awoke instantly.

"Things are happening, Charles," she said softly. "Better wake Eugene and take him over to the Findleys; Edith and Archie said to bring him anytime."

Hurriedly Dr. Mathias dressed, took Gene to the

neighbors and started up the old Buick coupé. Then he went back for Lillian.

"Here, let me carry you."

"No, Charles," protested his wife. "I can walk all right."

Driving as fast as he dared through the dense fog, Dr. Mathias arrived at the hospital, a mile and a half from his home, at 7:50 o'clock.

Dr. Kohn was scrubbed, ready and more than anxious.

"What kept you, Charles?" he asked. "Did you forget surgery was scheduled for 7:30?"

But Dr. Mathias only smiled. "I have another patient for you, doctor. Lillian's ready."

As Dr. Kohn quickly apologized, Mrs. Mathias was rushed to the delivery room.

Dr. Mathias was at her side, but as he prepared to wash his hands, Dr. Kohn brushed him aside. "This," he said, "is a case for steady hands."

Thereupon he delivered, five minutes later, a squawling, husky nine and one-half pound boy. When Dr. Mathias bent over his wife's bed, kissed her and whispered, "It's a boy," her arms encircled her husband's neck and drew him closer to her. Softly she sobbed: "Oh, Charles, I so wanted a girl." How could she have guessed that before he would be out of his teens that "repudiated" boy would make her the proudest mother in the world.

(Dr. Kohn has never forgotten his feat. Years later as president of the Tulare Rotary Club, he introduced Robert, just back from London, with this comment: "I guess my only claim to fame is that I was the first to spank this hero of heroes and swing him by his heels. But I'd sure hate to try it now.")

The baby was christened Robert Bruce and was an average infant in every way, though blessed with a more even temper than most. Though everyone else calls him "Bob," to this day he is still "Robert" to his parents. It is not a term of respect or special distinction. They merely believe in calling all their children by their Christian names.

Mrs. Mathias had to wait six more years to get her girl, for the next child was also a male, James. He arrived in January, 1934, and also has become quite an athlete in his own right. When Patricia finally put in her appearance in 1936, the family for whom fame lurked around the turn of a cinder track was complete.

When Bob is asked when he began to show his athletic genius, he demurs: "I never did anything different from any of the other kids—at least not until high school." But, here again he is being modest at the expense of accuracy. True, in his early years there were no foolproof indications that one day the entire globe would acclaim his track and field prowess, but in his development there were strong hints of future greatness to accompany the formation of a self-effacing character that would disarm any who might begrudge him his laurels.

His father was very soon impressed with Bob's coordination. He rarely fell from, or bumped into, furniture. Around the big oak tree on Apricot Street, the

15

base for the neighborhood moppets' activities, little Bob could "follow the leader" as well as his older playmates.

Just in time for Bob's fifth birthday party the family moved from Apricot Street to their present home, a rambling, Spanish style, white-stucco house which they had built at 790 East King Street, at the corner of Cherry Avenue. But when it was time for the party, Bob was nowhere to be found. Finally they located him under the bed, cutting his hair. He had been ashamed of its length and its tendency to curl, and he wanted to appear more manly before coming to the table.

Near the new house was a vacant lot in which, for years, the Mathias boys used to play. They had dug a cave in which they fixed up a clubhouse as a secret hideaway. It was a handy prop, too, for games of "Pirate" or "Cowboys and Indians." Also, they liked to roast potatoes in the intimacy of their hideout. Often they would light firecrackers and throw them into the cave and delight in the echo of the reverberating blast.

They were all normal youngsters, and Dr. and Mrs. Mathias did not want to restrain their healthy desire to romp in the fresh air. But because of the loose earth in the lot they feared the possibility of a cave-in. At last Mrs. Mathias called the boys together and explained the danger. "You wouldn't want one of your pals or yourselves to get hurt," she said. The boys agreed to give up their favorite haunt, but on one condition.

"We've gotta have a cave-filling ceremony," Gene, the spokesman for the brothers, said. So Mrs. Mathias trooped to the lot with them and after the mumbo jumbo of the proper rites, helped throw dirt into the cave and fill it up. That ended the Mathias family's association with the lot, but not before Bob, aged nine, had routed a neighborhood bully by skipping a rock off his head.

The scare he got over the cave caused Dr. Mathias to speed up the conversion of the backyard into an attractive recreation area for his family. The yard, measuring ninety by twenty feet, was roomy enough to allow the kids to play catch, run, wrestle, and in general work off their excess energy. Dr. Mathias also provided a gymnastic wonderland of bars, swings, horses and rings. Later he added a badminton net. He also put up a ping-pong table in the patio and in the basement fitted out a game room, dominated by a pocket-billiards table.

Dr. Mathias put no pressure on any of his boys to go out for school athletics, but he encouraged them along athletic lines as a means of wholesome diversion. Later he became team doctor for Tulare Union High and at meals the youngsters devoured almost as much sports gossip as they did food.

One of the most significant milestones in American sports history occurred the day Mrs. Mathias gave Gene, eight, and Bob, then five, two bronze medals their father had won in high school in Oklahoma. On one was inscribed Dr. Mathias' exploits as an all-purpose athlete, who played football and basketball and ran the 440-yard dash.

Bob was not exactly a sports "bug." He had no sports idol as a boy and read few sports books. But Gene was awed by the medals and aspired to "be like Dad." Bob, who took after his big brother, naturally did the same.

17

But when Gene began to bring some of his playmates into the yard to exercise, they did not want to be bothered with puny Bob.

"Make 'im scram," they ordered Gene. But Gene was reluctant. "Let 'im play just this once," he wheedled his chums.

Rather than waste time arguing, they ruefully agreed. But they found that Bob could throw a ball as hard and catch as well as they could. After that he was always one of the first to be picked when sides were chosen. "We kind of figured then that we had an athlete on our hands," Mrs. Mathias says.

While he looked up to his brother, Bob had a different nature. Gene was a promising student who liked science and nature and early determined to emulate his father's medical career. So did Bob, but in contrast to Gene, who was quieter and more conscientious, Bob was carefree and sprightly. In his early years he led as adventurous a life as any youngster in the hallowed tradition of the American small town.

Bob was not particularly attracted to books, but he learned to like to read when, during his grammar school years, he had to spend a lot of time in bed because of sickness. He never became a "bookworm," however, and he would josh himself as a "grind" whenever he brought home one of his infrequent "A's."

The first characteristic school incident his parents remember occurred when Bob was in the first grade at Wilson Grammar School. One day in late morning Mrs. Mathias was bustling about her housework when the phone rang. It was the first grade teacher.

18

"Now, Mrs. Mathias," she began in a harassed voice, "don't you worry, but Bob and another boy disappeared from class a little while ago—"

"Disappeared! My Robert?" Mrs. Mathias questioned. "But, how—"

"Well, we were playing games," the teacher explained, "and I was busy with another group of children, and when I looked around I noticed that Bob and another boy were gone from their group."

"But how? Where?" Mrs. Mathias stammered. "Are you sure? Have you looked all over the school?"

"Well, yes," the teacher answered. "But of course he may be hiding around here or something. Meanwhile, I'll look around some more and in case he shows up at home, you be sure to call me right away, and if I find him I'll phone back. Don't worry, Mrs. Mathias, he's probably around here close by."

Distraught, Mrs. Mathias ran out into the street to see if she could spot her son, but he was nowhere in sight. She started to walk toward the school nearby, but then she thought better of it and ran back into the house to telephone her husband. Before she did, she heard a familiar voice outside. She ran out and sure enough it was the hookey players, their arms intertwined about each other's shoulders.

Mrs. Mathias did not know whether to cry or scold. "Where have you been?" she demanded.

Bob was flustered but he had been trained to tell the truth. "Aw, Mom, we didn't want to play drop-the-handkerchief so we climbed out the window when teacher wasn't looking."

19

Bob got into a lot more mischief when he was six. On another occasion he and a friend, Bob Abercrombie, decided that the house of a neighbor, Frank Guerin, needed a new roofing job. They clambered to the top of the house and pulled off all of the old shingles.

"Now let's see where can we get some new ones," they were asking each other when Guerin appeared and put an abrupt end to their speculation.

Back on his home grounds, Bob enlisted three-year-old Jimmy's aid and went on a painting binge in his own house. This was the first time on record that he evinced a preference for the colors of the university he was later to attend. He and Jimmy got hold of some red paint and daubed the kitchen floor, the fruit jar cabinet, all of the fruit jars, the door, and were working on the walls when Mrs. Mathias burst in on them from her shopping trip.

"What on earth!" she cried. That permanently frightened the budding artists out of their talent for interior decoration.

Despite his athletic aptitudes and the manifold opportunities he had to perfect them, Bob in his first years took as much, if not more, joy in other pastimes. He loved to build things with his brothers. After they could no longer use the cave, they got together a few empty crates, a hammer and a sack of nails and built a clubhouse in their garage and then another in a nearby tree.

Once the brothers got an apple box, painted it, added four wire wheels and a steering bar, and used it as a cart. They named it "Doodle Bug." "It sounded like thunder going on the sidewalks," Mrs. Mathias relates, "but it lasted several years." The boys also constructed scooters with roller-skate wheels on which they zipped merrily around the neighborhood.

The Mathiases were only too glad to have their children's friends join them in the backyard. Despite the increased ruckus, everyone was welcome. "That way we knew where the children were," Mrs. Mathias says, "and we kept them off the streets." On weekends 790 East King Street became one of the busiest spots in town as the neighbors dropped in to chat and to watch the doings of their youngsters in the backyard. "It seems as if there was always a track meet or something going on back there," Mrs. Mathias says.

Whenever the gang did feel like trying more formal sports, requiring greater playing area, they were fortunate in having excellent facilities nearby. The high school field and gymnasium are only a block and a half from the Mathias residence and the playgrounds of Wilson Grammar School and Cherry Avenue Junior High School are within two blocks.

In their fun there were only two iron-clad rules by which the Mathias children had to abide. One was that they had to be back in the house by dark, and to assemble them Mrs. Mathias used to keep a loud whistle on a hook in the kitchen. Every evening about dusk she would step out on the back porch and blow it lustily as the signal for her youngsters to start home. The other rule, which Dr. Mathias insisted upon, was that all equipment borrowed from the backyard or game room had to be returned to its proper place when the children were through with it.

As Bob grew older he derived his greatest enjoyment from accompanying his father on hunting, fishing and hiking trips. To this day trout fishing remains his favorite pastime, though he no longer has much chance to pursue it.

Because they took after their dad in his love of the outdoors, the boys, for eight straight years, attended the YMCA summer camp at Tulequoia, situated about sixty miles from Tulare. Bob early became active in YMCA affairs, through school and the Methodist church. Later, in high school, Bob was to become a leader of the YMCA camp.

Bob joined the Cubs, but as most of their activities came during the summer, when he was away at camp, he did not go on to become a Scout. During his grammar school days Bob was not much attracted by sandlot sports. He still preferred other outdoor activities, particularly swimming.

Along with his brothers, he became an inveterate collector. When the family took a trip to Minnesota one year, so that Dr. Mathias could do some post-graduate study at the famous Mayo Clinic, the boys gathered thousands of book match covers. They also saved political campaign pins. They still have Landon and Wilkie buttons. The Mathias attic groans under the weight of twenty thousand pop bottle caps. Later they collected books about dogs, horses and, finally, doctors.

Then there was the marble craze. They saved "glassies" and "chalkies" and were always on the lookout to trade with their friends for rarely colored reds, blues or greens.

Meanwhile Bob branched out into a special sideline, collecting replicas of dogs. First he stocked up on the dime store, china variety. Then he added stuffed ones, plaster ones and whatever he could find. These figures can still be seen adorning the mantelpiece at home.

He built model airplanes and became interested in photography. Now whenever he goes on a trip his camera is as much a part of his kit as his track or football gear. His photograph album bulges with shots of the famous athletes he has competed against and the sites of those meetings, as well as the usual tourist snaps. Since going abroad, he has started to keep coins and hotel stickers from every country he has visited. In all of these hobbies he was encouraged by his parents, who felt it gave him interests that helped keep him out of trouble.

Like boys everywhere, Bob doted on pets. He raised hundreds of white mice and rats. His practice of collecting likenesses of dogs is explained by his special fondness for that animal. He repeatedly pestered his folks for puppies and at different times he has had Scotties, bird dogs, spaniels and bull dogs. Two of them were killed in accidents near the house, and in all there are five dogs buried in the backyard, each grave reverently marked with a white cross. Bob also has had as pets cats, rabbits, canaries, goldfish, parakeets, turtles, and even horses.

When Bob felt the need for pin money he earned it in the typical American junior's way—mowing lawns, picking fruit and helping on a friend's ranch. In addition there were the household chores at home. These rotated among the four children. Bob did his share, but he hated washing dishes; drying them, though, was O.K.

Then, after that day on the playground when he dared to take his first high jump at a level at which his brother had missed, sports began to intrude themselves more and more into his schedule.

Bob personally became interested enough in track and field to do some rehearsing on his own. Once he and a buddy, Richard La Marsna, set up a high jump bar in a neighbor's new bed of daffodil bulbs so that they would have a downy cushion when they landed. They had not done much jumping before the neighbor came storming out of the house, blue of face and with language to match. Thereafter Bob confined his practicing strictly to the playgrounds.

When he was eleven years old and in his last year at grammar school, Bob improved to five feet in the high jump and broad jumped fifteen feet. Though Bob possessed large, clumsy-looking feet, Bill Walker, his coach and a Tulare merchant, remembers: "There wasn't a kid in school who could keep up with him in the races." He also was class champion in the shot put.

By now the Mathias boys had taken to accompanying their father as he made the rounds of the hospital and called on his private patients. They did this not only because they liked to ride in the family car, but also because they were fascinated by their father's profession. There was such rivalry among them as to who should go along that to keep peace Dr. Mathias settled it by assigning them regular turns.

Often they would help him within the limits of their

youthful capacities, and they learned some of the technique and knowledge of his calling. Bob especially liked to hold an injured arm or leg when his father bandaged it or applied a cast. He became such an expert in medical terminology that by the time he was thirteen he knew the name of every bone in the human body.

He cluttered the bedroom he still shares with Jimmy with preserved tonsils, appendixes and other medical specimens. This intimate knowledge of anatomy has undoubtedly been a big factor in helping him to correct slight errors in form that when translated into terms of running, jumping and throwing spell the difference between an ordinary performance and a new record.

As the boys grew older, much of this collection was classified and sorted over until it took up less space. They hung basketball, football, and track jerseys, and school pennants on every inch of the walls. Bob rescued from a junk pile a sign reading: "Quitters never win and winners never quit." This he pasted in a spot where he could read it the first thing every morning.

Against the medical background of his family life, it is ironic that Bob Mathias' hardest struggle was not in the exhausting sport at which he became famous, the decathlon, but against a childhood disease that threatened permanently to undermine his health.

One day when he was still eleven years old, Bob came home from school, went up to his room and plopped down on his bed. His mother became worried and went up to see him. When she entered the room Bob was lying face up, with a handkerchief to his nose. He looked pale. It was disturbing that a boy who only a few hours ago had fought to avoid his afternoon nap should now lie down of his own free will instead of running out to play.

Mrs. Mathias sat down on the bed beside her son. "What's the matter, Robert?"

"Nothin', Mom, I'm just tired."

But that was too simple an answer to satisfy a doctor's wife. "Let me see that handkerchief." When she took it from him she saw it was stained with blood.

"When did this start?" she asked.

"Running home from school, I guess, Mom," Robert said.

Mrs. Mathias became very worried and when her husband came home she told him what had happened.

In his mind Dr. Mathias reviewed briefly his son's medical history. Some years before Bob had had his share of childhood diseases—whooping cough, chicken pox and a severe case of measles. In the fourth and fifth grades he had often complained that he was tired and he had been made to rest an hour when he came home from school before being allowed outside to play. For long stretches at a time he had been listless, without his usual pep. Now he was getting nose bleeds at the slightest exertion. Undoubtedly there had been an imperceptible weakening in his condition. He and his wife, preoccupied with the cares of raising a large family and earning a living, had overlooked the deterioration in Bob's condition.

The doctor took a blood count and found Bob deficient in red blood corpuscles. He was a victim of anemia.

Now Dr. Mathias had to move fast. He prescribed plenty of rest, including daily afternoon naps again, iron and liver pills, intermuscular shots and a vitamin-heavy diet. Bob had been a devotee of cow's milk since the age of six months, but now his parents literally poured it down him. He was also given huge amounts of orange juice and meat, and his hemoglobin began to build up.

But now Bob rebelled at the idea of having to rest like a "sissy" before going out to play. Yet that was probably the most important part of his cure. Before, when he was smaller and more easily managed, his mother had read to him and to some of his playmates who came into the house to "rest" with him. He never grew tired of listening to her read *Lassie,* and she bought for him all of Will James' Western stories and Terhune's dog stories, of which he was particularly fond.

But now he had outgrown that. He wanted to run with the gang. Mrs. Mathias feared he would hate her for making him lie down, but that was her husband's orders and, luckily, his word as "doctor" of the household was respected by all. Finally Mrs. Mathias' restless brain conceived a brilliant idea of how to help Bob relax and make it less of an onerous duty with him.

"Let's play a game, Robert," Mrs. Mathias said one day when her son came home from school. They went up to his bedroom. Bob lay down on his bed and Mrs. Mathias lay down beside him, on Jimmy's bed. "We'll both close our eyes and try to 'feel' ourselves relaxing," she said.

Bob did as his mother suggested. "My toes feel real

27

loose, Mom," Bob said after a while. He was trying hard to cooperate.

"I can feel my ankles getting real heavy," Mrs. Mathias said. "Just like they wanted to go to sleep."

"My knees feel real light," Bob said. "And my wrists are loose, and my fingers."

He's going too fast, Mrs. Mathias told herself. He wants to get it over with.

She stalled. "Robert, I can't seem to make my knees relax. How did you do it?"

"It's easy, Mom," Robert said. "Just don't hold 'em stiff. Just let 'em bend a little, natural. Don't you feel how light they get?"

Mrs. Mathias smiled. She had got him interested. It had worked. "By the time we had lain there thirty minutes," she recalls, "kidding ourselves into believing we actually could 'see' relaxation spreading over our bodies, we were really relaxed. And more often than not, either one or both of us were asleep. And that thirty minutes' nap for an eleven year-old was worth all the medicine in the world." Later, that ability to doze off easily was to prove one of the secret weapons in Mathias' athletic arsenal.

Bob's illness did not prevent him from improving at sports. He had only to be very much more careful of his personal habits than other youngsters. In the eighth grade he set a record by high jumping five feet, two inches.

When Bob entered high school the next fall he even participated in "B" football, but again his condition took a turn for the worse. He used to fall asleep in class.

His father stepped up his iron and liver shots, gorged him on milk, meat and vegetables, and ordered from ten to twelve hours of sleep a night. Bob was only a reserve in football and didn't see much action, and the fact that he was readily overcome by fatigue didn't hamper him. "I was only third or fourth string and didn't get to play much, so I really didn't feel it," Bob recalls.

Gradually Bob built himself up—he gives athletics a large part of the credit—and emerged from his weakened state. The following spring in track he was placed in Class C category, according to the regulations of the CIF (California Interscholastic Federation), the governing body of the state's prep athletics.

For his size he made a stellar showing. He high jumped 5 feet 5 inches; broad jumped 17 feet, 8 inches; put the eight-pound shot 49 feet, 4⅝ inches for a new county record; spun the light discus more than 100 feet; ran on the relay team and experimented with the hurdles.

In addition to all this he continued to take long outdoor trips and liked to help his brother Gene hunt birds' eggs. The latter, more versed in science, did most of the locating and spotting while Bob acted as retriever. Scrupulous about wildlife conservation, the boys devised a personal formula for their raids: "If there are five eggs, take three; if there are four, take two; if three, take one." If there were fewer than three eggs they would bypass the nest.

One day Gene diagnosed a real "catch" in a high tree that was difficult to climb. With Gene's help, Bob man-

29

aged to shinny up the trunk, and after a great deal of effort he found four prize eggs in a nest high up in the branches. Adhering to their code, he took two, put one in each side of his mouth so that he would have the free use of his arms, and started down.

When he got to the last branch he still was a good distance from the ground. He was tired and wanted the ordeal to be over with quickly.

On the ground Gene, seeing his brother flexing his knees for a jump, cupped his hands to his mouth and yelled: "Don't jump, Bob. Shinny down. I'll help you."

But it was too late. Bob had let go. He landed heavily and rolled over, and from the middle of the surprised look on his face, two baby birds popped out cheeping. Gene ran toward him, crying: "Are you hurt, Bob?" But when he saw what had happened, he doubled over in laughter. Bob, who had only been jarred by the impact of the fall, was disgustedly spitting out egg shells. "From now on, Gene," Bob pouted "you're going to have to hunt eggs alone."

Another talent which Bob exhibited was that of musician. Like other mothers, his own yearned to impart a bit of refinement to her fun-loving brood. She insisted on classical piano lessons. Bob didn't mind fooling with the keyboard, but he couldn't sit still for the classical themes and would have preferred to duck out and play.

Finally in high school he got a few lessons in popular music. He liked it. It was easier and more interesting. Bob became a great fan of the Ink Spots and started collecting dozens of their records, as well as other popular discs. He still keeps his hand in, playing the piano for his family or friends at home and for fellow athletes on trips. "But, it really doesn't sound like anything," he objects. He took up the clarinet in high school and tooted it in the high school band through his sophomore year. He also taught himself to pick out a few tunes on the guitar.

When Bob entered Tulare High his brother was a senior and already had established himself as a fine all-around athlete. Gene had suffered a head injury in football in his sophomore year that temporarily paralyzed his right side, but he had recovered to become a great basketball player and captain of the team and an excellent weight man in track.

Bob, who at fourteen was beginning to awaken to the marvelous flexibility of his body, worshiped his brother and again tried to imitate him. Typically the young man who is now the most versatile athlete living, says: "Shucks, I only went out for track in high school because my brother did."

Chapter 3

STARBURST

Bᴏʙ Mᴀᴛʜɪᴀꜱ ɢʀᴇᴡ ᴜᴘ ᴡɪᴛʜ ᴛʜᴇ ꜱᴜᴅᴅᴇɴɴᴇꜱꜱ ᴏꜰ ᴛʜᴇ cotton bolls coming ripe in the fields around Tulare.

With the proper rest and food and will power, Bob vanquished his anemia and put on six inches and forty pounds between his freshman and sophomore years of high school.

He stowed away tremendous quantities of meat, vegetables, fruit, milk and ice cream. He downed a quart of milk at each meal, another after coming in from his afternoon workout at the Tulare High field and two or three glasses as a nightcap. He ate almost everything except starches, the bane of good track performances, and tomatoes, for which he developed an unexplainable dislike.

The description of anemia, "pallor of the skin . . . shortness of breath and palpitation of the heart . . ." makes such a striking contrast with the subsequent relentless surge of a robust, tireless youth to an Olympic conquest against forbidding odds that Bob's recovery is one of the most remarkable in athletic annals.

Mathias grew so fast, in fact, that he outstripped the CIF's weight limit for Class B and, as he was not yet old enough for Class A, he had to forfeit his sophomore season of football.

He began to make up for lost time with the 1945–46 basketball season. As second-string varsity center he helped Tulare tie for its league championship.

During the 1946 track campaign, Bob first teamed with his six-foot, three-inch, 200-pound schoolmate Sim Iness—who also lost some his eligibility because he was too big—in an association that was to survive some boyish frustrations and eventually land them on the same Olympic squad, both as record-breakers.

"You'll notice the flying saucer reports started about the time Bob and Sim got serious about throwing the discus," Tulareans smugly point out.

Sim was more interested in baseball that spring until Fred Lugenbehl, who was aiding Head Coach Virgil Jackson handle the track team, talked him into trying the weights. He was much bigger than Bob, but he was not so far advanced in technique. However, he provided Bob spirited competition, and between them they harvested plenty of points in the strong-arm events.

Though still very much a novice, Bob also shone at the hurdles. And the improvement in his health gave free rein to the playful streak in his personality.

One day Mrs. Mathias returned to Tulare from a PTA (Parent Teacher Association) meeting in Sacramento and, because there was a track meet scheduled, went straight to the high school stadium. She arrived just as the hurdle race was finishing, but she was surprised to see that Bob wasn't even in it.

She turned to the student next to her. "Do you know why Bob Mathias wasn't in that race?"

The student looked at her with incredulous eyes. "What do you mean, wasn't in it?" He won it."

"Won it? But I'm his mother and I didn't see him out there."

"Oh," laughed the student. "Maybe you didn't know. He showed up in school today with his hair cut real short and bleached blond."

During the summer Bob added muscles by loading 100-pound sacks of sulphur into a plane that dusted crops in the area. When football season rolled around he almost made the fans forget his other talents, and he did it playing a position in which it is difficult to be impressive. Bob was stationed at right half in the modified double wing system employed by Jackson, whose main forte was football, but who doubled up to tutor the trackmen in the spring.

Mostly Bob was called upon to clear a path ahead of the ball carriers. He proved himself a devastating blocker, a deadly tackler and "play smeller" on defense, and in general an inspiring "team" player. Without doing much ball handling, Bob easily was the most outstanding gridder on the squad.

In one game with East Bakersfield High, the visitors' star halfback started a wide end run when Mathias, who saw the play coming, raced in from his linebacking position, crashed into the ball carrier ten yards behind the line with a resounding whack of leather, knocked him unconscious and broke his wrist.

Dr. Mathias, the team doctor, and Jimmy, who was mascot and water boy, rushed out onto the field. The doctor gave the injured player smelling salts and taped up his wrist. Jimmy threw a wet towel over his face. When the stricken lad opened his eyes and saw two familiar faces bending over him, he said: "Say, you Mathiases are pretty nice. One of you knocks me cold and two of you bring me around."

With that kind of rock and sock play, Tulare lost only one game that year.

Unkinking his football muscles, Bob quickly adjusted to the more sustained, cat-like action of basketball and won the varsity center position for the 1946–47 season. He promptly steered the Redskins, as all of Tulare's teams are called, into a tie for the league title. His long arms swept both backboards and owing to the spring his muscular legs had developed, he controlled most of the rebounds. (The biggest thrill of every game was to see Bob leap high into the air to grab a rebound, and with agile speed and perfect coordination of arms, legs, and body, dribble the ball into scoring territory.) On offense he contributed 81 points in eight conference tussles, the second highest total in the loop that season. On defense, his long arms and quick reflexes enabled him to steal many an opponent's pass.

He was getting so sharp on the hardwood that once his brother Gene suggested: "Say, Bob, why don't you forget about track and football and stick to basketball. You'd be a cinch All-American."

But Bob liked the variety of other sports too much to heed that advice. The spring of 1947 found him back on the cinders and in the pits, striving to improve his form, and his diligence returned sensational results.

In the first dual meet of the year Bob heaved the discus a respectable 135 feet, and his sidekick, Sim Iness, finished second with 133 feet. But their friendly rivalry was only warming up. They began to take firsts and seconds in the shot put as well, and all the while Bob kept getting better in the hurdles.

Then, just before one dual meet, Tulare's top high jumper was injured and Coach Jackson frantically searched his squad for someone who could substitute in the emergency. The meet was expected to be close and Jackson had been counting on those points. If the Redskins were shut out in the high jump, they could easily lose the meet.

With only one day of practice remaining, Jackson called a team meeting. "Who has had any high jumping experience?" he asked.

There was a dead silence. When he saw that no one else was volunteering, Mathias bestirred himself to answer. "I—I've had a little, coach," he said. "I haven't done it this year, but I did it last year in Class C."

"No one else?" Jackson demanded. Again silence.

"Okay, meeting's dismissed," he said. "Don't forget to read the blackboard for your instructions."

Jackson went over to Mathias. "Bob, I hate to ask you to do this. You've got enough to do already."

"That's okay Mister Jackson," Bob said. "Somebody has to do it. Only I don't know if I can go very high."

37

"How high have you done?"

"Well, last year I did five-five. Maybe I can do that again. I'll work on it now."

Jackson bit his lip. "Five-five? Well, if we're lucky, they won't get a clean sweep. Anyway, just do your best, Bob."

That afternoon, Bob sweated to regain his high jumping form. After his layoff, it was slow in returning. He got up to around five-six. Then it was dark and he had to quit.

The next day at the meet, after winning the hurdles and discus, he was called to the high jump pit. With only a brief warmup he had to begin jumping. He knew the outcome of the meet might well be riding on his shoulders and he was intent on not letting his teammates down. Up and up the bar went and still Bob remained in the running—five-six, five-eight.

Watching him, Jackson muttered in amazement: "He's doing it. He's coming through."

When the bar got to five-ten, only Mathias and one of his rivals was left. The other fellow missed all of his three tries. On his last jump Bob squared his jaw, stared unflinchingly at the bar, and zoomed over it. He had won. Jackson and some of the team members ran up to him and pounded him on the back. They had a hunch Bob might grab a point in the event but a victory was totally unlooked for. With this unexpected windfall, the meet was in the bag.

It was after that sensational display of versatility that Jackson first silently considered the possibility of his ace becoming a candidate for the decathlon. He himself knew very little about it, save that it required the diverse talents of a Mathias. The lesson of that meet was not lost on San Joaquin Valley fans and sports writers and they began to vocalize Jackson's unspoken sentiments.

As the season wore on, Bob ran up an unbeaten string in the hurdles and his discus rivalry with Iness waxed hotter. In the Tulare County championships the pair approached 140 feet and finished in the usual order. Finally, in the high school division of the Fresno Relays, Bob really set the stands abuzz with two meet records. He tossed the discus 140 feet, 6½ inches, and scorched the high hurdles in 14.6 seconds.

In the San Joaquin Valley CIF finals at Tulare a week later it was Iness who temporarily took over the limelight by unleashing a mighty 150-foot throw on his second attempt in the discus. No California schoolboy ever had attained that distance before. Mathias had one try remaining and calmly exhibited again his fabulous competitive spirit. He sailed the platter eight and one-half inches farther than Sim. That was too much of a blow for the latter, who muffed his final throw. The sure-fire parlay from Tulare had finished one-two again, but it was to take Iness a long time to get over the disappointment of losing a record so quickly.

In the high hurdles race at the same meet Bob was not so fortunate, though he did demonstrate his gameness. For the occasion Bob had wanted to get a new pair of track shoes, as his old ones were about to give out. But in the local stores he couldn't find a pair that fitted him. So he had to be content with taping up the

39

ones he had. On the sixth hurdle of the race he kicked a shoe off, but kept going anyway and finished fourth.

When the cheers of spring had trailed off into summer Bob continued to build himself up for future assaults on the record book. He worked again at loading sulphur sacks and did a lot of exercising in the backyard "gym." He ate heartily and got plenty of sleep. By fall he ranged six feet, one inch, weighed 190 pounds and was in the pink of condition for his final season of high school football.

Before the semester began, however, Tulare partisans got a scare when it was rumored that Iness, who was counted upon to plug one of the tackle slots and of course carry on the following spring in track, was dropping out of school.

The ostensible reason was that Sim had to go to work to help out his parents, struggling to make ends meet on their fruit ranch outside Tulare. But some of the sports-minded townsfolk, remembering Sim's disappointments of the previous spring, sensed that it might not be strictly a question of economics.

Prodded by Bill Walker, the boy's former coach, Si Tyler, agreed to sound out Iness. The still-growing behemoth was evasive about the reason for his not returning. Si suspected a problem of morale and, as Tulareans often do in a crisis, beelined for the Mathias residence.

After a family huddle, it was announced that Bob would not compete in the discus next spring in order to concentrate on other events. Bob denies this gracious act of self-denial, but the following season he actually did ease off in the discus. Bob says he did this only to help the team gain more points. With the capable Iness taking care of the discus, Bob said he would perfect himself in his other specialties and thus make a greater contribution to the scoring. But undoubtedly Bob was moved by the desire to do everything that could in the remotest way influence his friend to continue his education.

Whatever it was that persuaded Sim to change his mind contributed no little to a great sports year for Tulare High. With Iness safely installed at tackle and Mathias, the team captain, switched to tailback, the Redskin gridders got away to a roaring start. Before they took off their pads for the last time they had provided their followers with more thrills than any Tulare squad in a long time.

As expected, Bob excelled at his new post. Barging into opposing lines with the authority of a tractor and flitting like a hare in the open field, he averaged more than eight yards a carry, scored fourteen touchdowns—five in one game—and assisted on three others. He gained 1,268 yards from running and passing, more than all Tulare's regular season foes combined.

He passed thirty-eight times, connecting on eighteen for 350 yards, for an average of about twenty yards a throw. He amassed 418 yards on kick returns, three of which he took into the end zone after dashes of ninety-five, sixty-seven and fifty-five yards. Against a traditional rival, Porterville, he broke loose for scoring scampers of twenty-two, seventy, and sixty-one yards. "It got so," one Tularean recalls, "that they practically gave up trying to stop him. They just let him through—

peaceful-like." Mathias had two other long touchdown runs of ninety and sixty-eight yards nullified by penalties.

In addition, he kicked off, placekicked and punted. And, while it hardly seems possible, some claimed him to be a greater defensive than offensive player. He made tackle after tackle, gummed up most of the opposition's pet stratagems and averaged almost fifty minutes of playing time in each contest.

Tulare lost the playoff for the San Joaquin crown to powerful Roosevelt High of Fresno, 20-13, but its magnificent regular season showing and Mathias' all-league honors were solace enough. Valley fans rate him the finest back produced in their area since Red Strader, former St. Mary's College star and coach of the now-defunct New York Yankees, shone for Modesto High in the early 1920's.

Jackson, who schooled him in both sports, still deems Mathias a greater football player than trackman. He feels strongly on this matter, for Bob's absence the following year practically cost him his job. Tulare lost every game and, under mounting pressure, Jackson lost his position. "Bob Mathias was the greatest thing that ever happened to me," Jackson said. And to prove it he named his son Glenn Mathias Jackson, in honor of his greatest pupil.

Shortly before the 1947 football season ended, Dean Cromwell, the veteran USC track coach, who was to lead the American Olympic squad the following summer, came to Tulare to address a combined luncheon of Trojan alumni and Tulare clubmen.

He told the gathering, "You have a boy here who can, if he wants, make the United States Olympic track team next summer as a decathlon man." But he cautioned Bob, whom he described as a "terror," that he should give up football and basketball if he wanted to became an expert in the decathlon.

Bob, however, did not take the suggestion seriously and had too much school loyalty to refuse to participate on two varsity teams of which he was a key member.

When Jackson himself first broached the idea of the boy's training for the decathlon, Bob still was not much interested. He knew even less about the event than his coach. To influence him Jackson said: "Bob, you're the best athlete I've ever seen." Knowing Bob so well, he was not afraid the boy would develop a swelled head and he risked a prediction. "If you start training hard now, you might have a chance to make the 1952 Olympic squad."

How the Tulare marvel telescoped that prediction into a success story of four weeks instead of four years makes drama to compare with anything that sports has provided since the Golden Twenties.

Chapter 4

BOY MEETS DECATHLON

BEFORE TAPPING HIM ON THE SHOULDER, DESTINY GOT only a shrug from Bob Mathias.

Instead of heeding Dean Cromwell's advice to lay off basketball in the winter of 1947–48 and concentrate on decathlon events, Bob played the hardwood sport with more zeal than ever before. He knew little about the decathlon and cared even less. The Olympics were still far off; basketball was here and now, and he was team captain. In a fitting farewell as a prep cager, he averaged eighteen points a game and was an All-San Joaquin Valley selection at center.

Bob could have scored more points, but he was too generous to score more than necessary. One night at a Tulare home game, the locals took a commanding lead in the second half and Bob's point output dropped sharply. In the stands a friend nudged Gene Mathias and asked: "How come Bob isn't scoring?"

"Isn't scoring? Watch him—he won't even shoot, he'll just feed the ball to someone else," Gene said. "When we get so far ahead, Bob just quits trying for points. He doesn't see any sense in hogging all the scoring for himself."

College talent scouts began besieging Tulare. One day a basketball coach from a certain university was walking in the street when he drew up short at seeing a familiar face approaching him. It was the football coach from the same school. "What are you doing here?" he demanded.

"I've come to talk to this kid Mathias," the football coach said.

The basketball mentor blinked. "Why didn't you tell me he was an all-arounder? I could have saved myself some train fare."

But Bob was too busy to think much about college, and Dr. Mathais tried to discourage the ivory hunters. He told one: "I want Robert to go to school with no strings attached. Let them give the scholarships to boys who can't afford to pay their own way." Gene already was in Stanford, and Bob had tentatively decided to follow him if his grades were good enough.

Bob's reputation in high school was composed as much of personal honesty as it was of athletic ability; and he was elected senior class president, secretary-treasurer of the high school YMCA club, and treasurer of the lettermen's society, even though he still got a bit tongue-tied when making a speech.

His schoolwork Bob has always taken seriously, but he tends to regard it almost as a necessary evil. In high school he took full advantage of the scheduled study periods and got most of his homework done during them.

In track, led by its seasoned duo of Mathias and Sim

Iness, Tulare again swept victoriously through its dual meet slate. Bob finished his second straight regular season unbeaten in the hurdles. Over his entire high school career he had won forty first places and broken twenty-one records, an accomplishment probably unmatched anywhere in prep competition of equal caliber.

In the high school division of the Fresno Relays that May, Tulare led all other entrants with twenty-seven points. These were accounted for by Mathias' 54-foot shotput, a new meet record; his 14.6 seconds victory in the high hurdles, equalling his own Relays standard set the previous year; his second place in the high jump with a leap of over six feet; and Iness and Mathias finishing in that order in the discus. Iness' throw of 148 feet, 6¼ inches, eclipsed Bob's old Relays record.

Mathias did so well in all of the events he entered that Coach Jackson insisted his ace think seriously about the decathlon. "I don't know much about it, Bob," Jackson told him, "but I know you have to be able to do a lot of things well. I think it's made to order for you."

Bob still was rather cool toward the idea. He toed the ground with his spikes. "Gee, I don't know," he said. "I wouldn't know where to begin."

"Tell you what," Jackson said. "There are a lot of decathlon guys here at the meet—Gay Bryan, Al Lawrence, Jerry Shipkey, Floyd Simmons. Why don't you talk to them and find out something about it?"

Bob looked up, alarmed. "Me talk to all those big college athletes? Gee, I don't know—"

However, Jackson overcame Bob's fears and together

47

they sought out the quartet. When Bob was introduced and shook hands, he blushed, fidgeted and mumbled: "Gee, it sure is swell meeting you."

The older athletes had applauded Bob's exploits among the preps, and they were eager to help. But when they heard that he wanted a briefing on the decathlon they could not avoid being skeptical. They hated to discourage him, yet they could not help feeling that he was overreaching himself.

"Does this kid know what he's getting into?" they wondered. "Oh, well, if we just give him the facts he'll see the light and forget about it."

Briefly they recited the facts. "There are ten events, spread over two days. Olympic rules say it must end by midnight of the second day, no matter what. On the first day you do the 100-meter dash, the broad jump, the 16-pound shot, the high jump and the 400-meter run. The second day, the 110-meter high hurdles, the discus, pole vault, javelin and 1,500-meter run.

"Most of the events work against each other. You go all-out in the 100 meters and you're tired, but you've got to come right back and run hard in the broad jump. Your legs take a terrific beating landing in that pit. You can catch your breath a little in the shotput, but you have to wait around a long time between turns and you can get cold and lose your spring for the high jump. Then, after all that kicking and straining, you've got to sprint all the way in the 400 meters.

"You score points according to how well you do against a certain standard. Right now it's the 1934 world record or the Olympic record, whichever is best.

If you equal the record in an event, you get a thousand points. It's scaled on down from there.

"You've really got to know how to pace yourself. You don't get anything for winning a heat. It's strictly your time that counts. If you win a race and your time is slow, you might not score as much as a guy who finishes way back in a faster heat. In a field event it's sometimes better to skip your last try if you feel the extra rest will help you score more points in the next event. It's like being in a private track meet—you must always keep adding up your points and you're practically your own coach and trainer, too. At the end of two days you'll ache all over and feel as dizzy as a squirrel running inside a wheel. You'll swear 'never again' but by then you may be so far gone you'll want to have another go at it. That's about it."

Bob thanked them absently and walked away, deep in thought. "Boy, the more I hear of the decathlon, the less I like it," he said to himself. "But Jackson seems to think I can do it and he's a pretty smart coach. I'll see."

The Southern Pacific Regional AAU games were scheduled for Pasadena in a few weeks, and were to include a decathlon to help screen local Olympic aspirants in that event. Jackson pointed Bob for this meet.

"It'll do you good to be in that kind of competition," Jackson told him, "and you'll have a chance to rate yourself in the decathlon. Then you'll know how many points you'll have to improve. By 1952 you will have had the benefit of expert college coaching, and if you keep at it I'll bet you can make the Olympics then."

"I'll see what I can do," Bob promised.

But he was faced with so many serious problems in preparing himself that a less wholesomely naïve character would have thrown up his hands in surrender. Not only was he totally unacquainted with some events of the decathlon, but other important matters would cut deeply into what little time remained. Bob had to keep practicing his regular specialties for the CIF track finals at Berkeley in two weeks and he could not afford to ease up in his studies if he wanted to be graduated in June.

Back in Tulare once more Bob boned up on the metric system of measurement, which is used in the decathlon, and got a book from the school library that told something about the ten-phase event. But it wasn't much help. He had to have the practice, and he never had held a javelin, or pole vaulted, or run a 400 meter or a 1,500 meter race. He had only broad jumped and sprinted infrequently. Even in the familiar hurdles he was at a disadvantage. In CIF meets the high hurdles are only 39 inches off the ground, instead of 42, as they are in college-level competition.

To make up that difference Jackson nailed slats across the top of the high school's hurdles. Bob had to master the higher lift, but he also could not afford to forget the timing at the lower height for use in the forthcoming CIF championships.

When it came to practicing the javelin, an event banned by the CIF, Bob and his coach were really stunned. They couldn't locate a javelin in all of Tulare county. Jackson had to send to Los Angeles for one and, at the same time, he ordered a decathlon guide.

Even when the javelin arrived, there was little Jackson could teach Bob about it. He later confessed to Jack McDonald, a San Francisco sports editor, that he wasn't much of a track coach. "Like a lot of high school coaches in cities the size of Tulare, I'm just sort of a jack of all trades and master of none," Jackson told McDonald. "I'm primarily the football coach and sort of double in brass as track coach in the spring. I just do the best I can with what little knowledge I have."

He could teach Mathias the rudiments of the shot and discus, but the basketball coach at Tulare, Ernie Lambrecht, was a hurdler at Chico State, and he gave Jackson a hand with Mathias whenever he could.

Aided by what these men could show him and by his own ready grasp of form and his quick intelligence, Bob began to experiment with the unfamiliar arts of the decathlon.

He took the javelin home with him and at first, with the decathlon guide and a track manual open beside him, just practiced gripping it. Then he began to drive it into the ground a few feet in front of him. On the regular field he gradually lengthened his throws, but he had not gone far before he had to leave off and give most of his attention to the pole vault.

The first week he vaulted, Bob had difficulty clearing eight feet. After the bamboo had fallen on him from that height time and time again, Bob looked imploringly up at his coach from the pit and, spitting sawdust, said: "Whew! This is even tougher than the javelin!"

Jackson wondered, "Is he going to quit?" He tried to

think of something to say that would show appreciation of the difficulty. "Pretty tough coming down, huh, Bob?"

"That isn't so tough," Bob cracked. "It's the getting up that's hard."

Bob had the requisite speed afoot and gymnasts' muscles rippled in his back, and he wasn't easily discouraged. Gradually he attained the respectable height of 10 feet but could not go much further before he had to take time out from his labors to represent Tulare in the State finals.

That meet, drawing three hundred of the classiest schoolboy tracksters to be assembled anywhere, was to provide Bob with a mild prevue of the trying weather conditions he was to encounter in the future.

After the first two events had been run off on a dry oval, a spring drizzle descended on Edwards Field, track plant of the University of California in Berkeley, just as the barriers were being put out for Mathias' first show, the 120-yard high hurdles. It bothered some of the other colts, but fazed Bob not a bit. Despite the heavy going, the fleet competition inspired him to the best clocking of his life, 14.5 seconds, as he won the race by a foot.

Later, with the rain still slanting down, Bob came back in the 180-yard low hurdles to win easily by nine yards in 19.6 seconds. He was the meet's only double winner, and he hoisted little Tulare to fourth in the team standings, trailing only three big Los Angeles area schools.

A second sight of that golden blur of brown hair, maroon jersey and suntanned skin ruffling the clean white tape so moved the announcer that he began drooling superlatives. As Bob ascended the stand for the victory presentation, the loudspeaker trumpeted: "America's greatest hope in the decathlon."

Few in the stadium took the pronouncement seriously, least of all Mathias. He knew that even to make a respectable showing at the Pasadena games, which were almost upon him, he must cram in every extra minute of practice he could.

Back to work he went, on the infield and around the track. He tried to improve his javelin and pole vault form. In the broad jump he had to brush up on his step and takeoff, neglected since grammar school days. His thigh muscles shrieked their protest as he stretched for the higher hurdles. In the flat races he had to learn pace, something he had not been too concerned about before.

The discus had always been his favorite, but he had not thrown it as much this year, and he had to renew the feel. The high jump meant more tugging and falling and savoring sawdust. He always had been strong in the shotput, but now he had to fling the 16-pound shot, and his upper arm, not heavily knotted, groaned under the added four-pound burden.

Such were Bob Mathias' problems when the personally humble but athletically brash young man had to end his rehearsing and, accompanied by his coach, depart for his first official crack at the decathlon. Before they left Tulare, Coach Jackson told his wife: "Well, Bob's in the big leagues now, but I've got a funny hunch he will do all right."

The favorite at Pasadena was Lawrence, the USC speedster, whom Southland scribes were touting as the most dangerous challenger to national decathlon champion Irving (Moon) Mondschein. Also highly regarded were Jerry Shipkey, UCLA weight specialist, and Floyd Simmons, former North Carolina star, who had moved to Los Angeles. The presence of the seventeen-year-old Mathias among the more experienced club and college veterans was looked upon as little more than a novelty.

As the meet got underway, however, the experts quickly had to revise their opinions. First, Lawrence hurt his ankle and was forced to the sidelines. Shipkey looked off form. Mathias, a bit baffled by all the frenzied arithmetic, nevertheless held steady midst the strange goings-on. He posted better than average performances in all the first day's events: 11.3 seconds in the 100 meters; more than 21 feet in the broad jump; 43 feet in the shot; 5 feet, 10 inches in the high jump; and 52.1 seconds in the 400 meters. After the last race, in which he did his best ever, he surprisingly found himself with a five-point lead over Shipkey.

The eyebrows of the writers arched in salute. "What gives? Is this lazy looking kid gonna take it? Every time you look at him he's wrapped in his blanket, asleep. Naw, he can't last."

But the next day Bob turned in a decent 15.7 seconds set of hurdles and whipped the discus 140 feet and clung gamely on top. Then came the pole vault. With the bar at nine feet, six inches, he missed. "I'm tiring," he thought. "I'll relax and make it next time." But he also flubbed his next chance. Up until now the little worrying he had done had been about the 1,500 meters. He had never run the full distance in practice. But now, if he missed on his last pole vault, he would face oblivion before he ever got to the metric mile.

True, the pole vault had given him the most trouble, but he had previously cleared ten feet. "What am I doing wrong?" Bob asked himself. Before his last try came around he decided to approach Dick Nash, a Los Angeles track official who was helping supervise the vaulting.

"Mister Nash, I'm having trouble getting my step," Bob said. "I wonder if . . ."

Nash had followed with admiration the unheralded youngster's plucky fight and he anticipated his predicament. He tried to steady him with a smile: "Sure, you want to work out your step on another runway? Okay, go over there and I'll call you in time for your turn."

Bob went to the indicated strip and tried a few practice runs. When Nash called him, he felt he was ready. Sure enough, he cleared the bar with more than a foot to spare on his third try. Then he continued higher than he had ever gone before, 11½ feet. It had been a close call, but it also proved to be the turning point of the day.

In the next activity, the javelin, Mathias could not exceed 155 feet on his first two tosses. The more seasoned Shipkey, still close behind, rallied and sailed one out 170 feet. "I guess that'll hold the boy wonder," he grinned. But he was to gag on those words the next time Mathias unwound. Again rising to the occasion, Bob shot the spear 171 feet, another all-time best for him.

If he could tour the 1,500 meters in only fair time,

55

Bob appeared a certain winner. Tulare's pride was woozy by now, but he didn't fail. He broke five minutes and while, relatively, it was his poorest event, he finished with 7,092 points to complete his stunning upset. What's more, it was the highest decathlon score made in the United States since 1941. When it was over, Bob knew that the description of the decathlon he had first heard at the Fresno Relays was no exaggeration.

Back home, among his family and friends, he said: "Yeah, I sure was surprised, but you should have seen Jackson—he was speechless."

Having come this far, Bob naturally decided to enter the national decathlon championships, which also serve as the Olympic tryouts and were scheduled for June 25 and 26 at Bloomfield, New Jersey. While the initial victory of the untried teen-ager was hailed as a remarkable achievement, authorities were quick to point out that, after all, he had not yet met the kingpin, Mondschein, three-time U.S. decathlon champion. That would be the true test, they said.

When the field of twenty-two of America's jack-of-all-track-trades gathered at Foley Field, Bloomfield, June 25, it was Mondschein, a 24-year-old Pacific War vet and ace high jumper from New York University, who naturally ruled as a big favorite. Lawrence, recovered from his injury, and Simmons also were rated threats. Mathias had aroused interest by his recent triumph on the Coast, but though he had tallied more points than Mondschein had in taking the title in 1947, no one took his chances very seriously—except maybe Mathias and a couple of his avid Tulare fans who were at the meet.

With the opening gun Mondschein looked unbeatable. He got off his finest first-day performance ever, garnering 4,187 points or only five less than Glen Morris had made en route to his world's record of 7,900 in the 1936 Olympics. The wags nodded their heads knowingly. The kid from Tulare was only third, with 3,833, trailing Simmons by 52 and Mondschein by 354.

Bob's time of 11.2 seconds in the 100 meters had lagged Mondschein by a tenth of a second. The defending champ had been tops in the broad jump with a leap of over 23 feet, while the best Bob could do was 21 feet, 6 inches. Bob's shotput of 42 feet, 6 inches, was third longest, but Mondschein was right behind. In the high jump, his specialty, Mondschein soared 6 feet, 5 inches, to lead the pack, while Bob cleared 6 feet. In the 400 meters, Bob's 51 seconds flat was a tenth of a second slower than the NYU star's time.

At the midway point, S. B. (Si) Tyler, secretary-manager of the Tulare Elks club, who was taking motion pictures of Bob's doings at Bloomfield, approached Mathias with a look of concern on his face. "I'd hate to see you lose this," he said.

But Bob was no longer the complete novice. He had gotten a big brown decathlon scoring book of his own and was coolly calculating his chances like all the rest. "Don't worry," he shot back. "I don't think I'll lose. My best events are tomorrow anyway."

The next day threatening clouds hung over Foley Field as competition resumed. Bob had already proven himself a good mudder, and he didn't much care. In the hurdles he chased Lawrence across the line with a fast

15.1 seconds performance that earned him more than 900 points. Mondschein was far back. In the discus Bob neared 140 feet and picked up almost 800 more points. The best Mondschein could do was 125 feet and he saw his lead dwindling. Moreover, he complained of a sore arm.

Then the thunderstorm broke and made a travesty of the affair. As athletes, judges and spectators scurried for cover, the rain beat down for an hour and a half, turning the track and the infield into a quagmire. When it finally let up and the session got going again, most of the competitors were down in the mouth. Mathias was just beginning to enjoy himself.

The pole vault, next on the agenda, was rendered an almost physical impossibility by the gooey runway. Lawrence, who had cleared 13 feet previously, couldn't hold the wet pole and went no higher than 11 feet, 6 inches. Bob refused to give way and tied him at that height. Mondschein was slipping fast.

The javelin path, too, was a slimy streak of mud, but Bob's big feet gave him plenty of traction and he got off a toss of more than 157 feet, fifth highest in the event. Mondschein was not even among the first ten in the spear, and the two were now neck and neck in the scoring.

In the final event, the metric mile, Bob cut seven seconds off his previous best and came home the winner by a margin of 123 points. His winning total of 7,224 was the highest made in the world since 1940. Mondschein was second with 7,101 and Simmons third with 7,054. Headed by the amazing 17-year-old kid, this was the trio that would represent the United States in the Olympic decathlon.

Tyler was so carried away by the triumph that he made the first unofficial bid to AAU officials to bring the national decathlon championships to Tulare the next year.

Tulare first got word of its favorite son's success when the teletype clacked out a flash in the offices of *The Advance-Register*. The news quickly spread through the downtown area, setting off the first of a famous series of impromptu Mathias victory celebrations. People stopped each other in the streets and exchanged congratulations. There was a happy gathering at the Mathias house, where the local radio station was interviewing the beaming parents.

"I'm thrilled to death," the impassive Dr. Mathias said. But the more excitable Mrs. Mathias could hardly contain herself. All she could shout into the microphone was: "Bob's the decathlon champion of the United States!"

Back in Bloomfield, getting ready to fly home for a brief rest before the Olympics, Bob was unaware of the commotion he had caused. After the meet, Bob telephoned home and, at the end of the conversation, when his mother asked him if there was anything she could do for him, he replied, innocently, "Yes, Mom. Would you mind driving over to the airport to meet me, so I won't have to take the bus home?" The unspoiled kid who had just made the Olympic team in sensational fashion had not even assumed that his parents would meet him, let alone that some of the townsfolk were

59

planning a motorcade to escort him the nine miles from Visalia airport to his home.

When Bob returned and his father noticed that his old track shoes had practically disintegrated from the heavy duty at Bloomfield, he decided to go to Los Angeles and buy his son a pair to wear next month at London.

When he entered a large sporting goods store, Dr. Mathias was met by a smiling, eager clerk. "I'd like to buy a pair of track shoes," the doctor said.

"Fine, sir," the clerk responded. "What size do you want?"

"Thirteen," Dr. Mathias answered.

The clerk, thinking his customer was mistaken and not wanting him to go away with a purchase he would have to return, asked: "Pardon me, but how old is the boy?"

"Seventeen," said the doctor. "Why?"

"Seventeen!" The clerk threw his hands in the air in resignation. "Friend, if he's only seventeen and takes a size thirteen shoe, he's too clumsy ever to be an athlete. Take my advice and save your money."

The same day Bob Mathias enplaned for London, he had an hour's visit with Edwin M. Sweet, pastor of Tulare's First Methodist church. Rev. Mr. Sweet later told his congregation: "I called upon the heavenly Father to give Bob strength, not necessarily to win, but to give of his best and under all conditions to give a good witness for his Master."

Chapter 5

THE OLYMPIC FLAME

EVEN AFTER BOB MATHIAS' GREAT VICTORY IN THE NA-tional championships under adverse weather condi-tions, some had doubt as to his ability. The attitude of the track experts seemed to be: "Up until now he's been lucky. He's never been out of the country. Wait until he gets up against that tough international competition on a foreign field and with foreign officials. Then we'll see how he stands up under the strain. You've got to be a lot older and wiser in the Olympics. Maybe next time."

In an interview on the liner carrying the American team to England, Ward Haylett, Kansas State Coach who was assigned to supervise the decathlon men, told the press: "Mathias shows great promise, but I'm not ready to assume that he can beat Mondschein again. Don't forget, Mondschein was bothered by a sore arm in the field events on the second day of the Bloomfield tryouts. But I'll work hard with Bob and he can prob-ably improve his marks."

However, Bob was having too much difficulty getting accustomed to the ocean to bother about what was being said or written about him. The first couple of days out he was sick, and he had trouble getting enough rest and staying in condition.

He was sharing a stateroom with Mondschein and Simmons and the first night he was fitfully slumbering when the lights flashed on at three in the morning, waking him.

Mondschein was up and hopping around.

"What is it, lifeboat drill?" Bob asked, anxiously.

"Nope," Mondschein dead-panned. "Calisthenics."

The swarthy NYU grad kept that up the whole way over and Mathias and Simmons couldn't figure out if he was trying to set an example for them, or whether he thought the added exercise would help improve the score he made at Bloomfield, or whether he was just kidding. But Bob didn't get much sleep and he was very glad when the boat finally docked.

Along with those of twelve other nations, Uncle Sam's male athletes were quartered at Uxbridge, a RAF station ten miles from Wembley Stadium, site of the games, which had been taken over and renovated to serve as one of the Olympic villages.

The barracks had been repainted yellow with blue trimmings, and the competitors slept four to a room. Tons of American food were flown in daily, including fresh bread every morning. Even hometown newspapers were provided. The station had a practice track and other training facilities. It also was equipped with dental, medical, and physiotherapy clinics; a bank, post office, movie, barber shop; and dry cleaning, tailoring, and laundry services.

After workouts began, many of the athletes began to avail themselves of most of these facilities and went sight-seeing as well. But not Bob. The fun could come after. The honor of representing his country was not to be taken lightly. Although at seventeen he was one of the youngest members of the United States squad, no one took his training more seriously. Pitted against thirty-seven of the finest physical specimens from nineteen countries, Bob realized that he would have to make proper use of every moment before the decathlon opened. Furthermore, almost his entire family was coming 6,000 miles to see him and he did not want their trip to be in vain. He hoped, with luck, to place third and at least take home a medal.

Bob trained so hard, in fact, that he incurred a couple of painful injuries that would further handicap him in the mankilling cycle he was about to attempt. While throwing the javelin, with which he was still unfamiliar, he injured an elbow. "What I really need is a javelin with jet propulsion," he joked. Then after many jarring landings in the unyielding white sand of the British high jump and pole vault pits, his knee began to swell.

Although his injuries forced him to cut down somewhat on the ambitious training schedule he had set for himself, he showed improvement in many events. Coach Haylett predicted: "The way he's going now he'll score 7,400 points." That would make him a serious contender, but there still was a lot of skepticism about the ability of this smooth-cheeked, willing, and likable boy to place high in what was probably the strongest international decathlon field ever assembled.

But then there was no longer time for speculation. The first day of competition dawned—rainy and cold.

That August 5th Bob arose at seven A.M., drank some orange juice and wolfed down a steak, then boarded the bus for Wembley Stadium. There he dressed and warmed up on a practice field since the competitors were not allowed to tune up in the stadium itself.

Despite the rain, 70,000 of the sport-loving British and foreign guests packed the stands.

At ten o'clock Mathias was called for his first event, the 100-meter dash. By now the dampness had caused two entrants to drop out and the field was cut to thirty-five. Bob was not completely warmed up yet, but he managed to win his heat in a fast 11.2 seconds sprint— a good start. Enrique Kistenmacher, a big, good-looking Argentine army lieutenant whose face was darkened by the perpetual knit of his fierce black eyebrows, did 10.9 seconds, however, and took the lead in points.

The broad jump was next. Bob concentrated on doing everything right. He ran hard, got a lot of spring into his legs at the takeoff board and hurtled forward to the best distance he had ever recorded, 23 feet. But he couldn't hold his balance and fell back, losing a few feet. It was a tough blow.

He put his sweat clothes back on and had to wait in the wetness while the thirty-four others took their turns. It was an hour before his second jump came around. He was stiffer by now and leaped only 21 feet, 8 inches. He could not better that on his third try and slipped further off the pace being set by Kistenmacher, who broad jumped more than 23 feet. Ignace Heinrich of France also got off a good jump and passed Bob to take over second place. It was evident that he, too, would prove difficult to overhaul.

Next on the program was the shotput. Again Bob set himself to deliver his best. He had to if he was going to catch up. On his first effort he put everything he had into the toss and pushed the steel ball out to the 45-foot mark. As he stepped forward out of the circle a smile of satisfaction crossed his face. But it was quickly wiped off by the waving of the red flag, indicating a foul. Bob was stunned.

"What's wrong?" he demanded of the official. "I stayed in the ring while I threw."

"Yes, but when you finished you didn't step back of that line through the middle of the circle," the official said.

"But why?" Bob asked. "I never heard of that."

"It's the rule," the official replied, his patience obviously strained.

"But nobody told me," Bob persisted. He seldom got wrought up, but he felt he was being treated unfairly.

"I'm sorry," the official said and turned his back to signify that the argument was over.

Bob walked disconsolately away. "There go more points," he mused. Even so his subsequent toss of 42 feet, 9 inches was better than either Kistenmacher or Heinrich could do, and he gained slightly on both. But he knew that in the final reckoning the foul could spell the difference between a medal and an also-ran.

In the next event, the high jump, Bob determined to make up for his disappointment in the shotput. After all, the high jump had been one of his strong points in high school. As he awaited his call, seated on a folding chair, wrapped in a blanket against the rain and studying his big brown scoring book, he was approached by his brother Gene, who was communicating between the Mathias family in the stands and its representative on the field.

Spectators were not allowed on the field but Gene was using an old press pass the British were mysteriously honoring. He had come by it at the California State meet, where it had been discarded by this writer. Gene pocketed it with the idea it might do him some good at London. And he was correct. At that time he did not know the writer and vice versa, but, ironically, the discarded pass contributed, if only in the remotest way, to the success of the family's trip.

"How's it going, Robert?" Gene asked when he came up to his brother on the field. "You worried?"

Bob shrugged his shoulders. "What's the use? They don't give points for worrying."

He snuggled in his blanket and tried to concentrate on the book. But something was wrong. His knee and his elbow throbbed. He reflected that maybe the "wise guys" were right. He had not known before anything like Olympic pressure, battling every step of the way against the best in the world. When he looked up through the rain at the stands he saw that 70,000 pairs of eyes were fixed on his every move.

With the high jump bar at 5 feet, 9 inches, Bob lunged and knocked it off. He was puzzled. "What did I do wrong?" he questioned. He couldn't decide for sure. "Oh well, I'll make it next time." He huddled under the blanket again and tried to rest.

The next time his name was called he stepped determinedly in front of the pit, eyed the bar, squared his jaw, shivered ever so slightly in the chill wind and took off. He gathered speed, kicked his right leg high, tucked the left one under—and knocked off the bar again.

As he picked himself up from the pit, Bob sighed audibly. His face was mud-streaked, and perspiration beaded his brow. Head down, he walked over to where his sweat clothes were. As he slowly put them on, he stared at the wet ground. Some of the grass blades at his feet seemed to swim into the shape of jagged letters, spelling out a word: *Failure*. With an effort he pulled away his eyes and looked up. He took a deep breath, walked over to his chair and sat down.

He tried to freeze the action of the last jump in his mind so he could discover the spot where he had gone wrong, but his brain felt as logy as his body. Yet often in high school he had cleared the same height with ease. It was beyond understanding.

He put his elbows on his knees, interlocked his arms and rested his head on them. Swathed in the darkness of the blanket, he tried to forget where he was. It had worked for him before. He had to shut out the meet, the crowd, everything.

"Don't worry, don't worry," a small voice kept repeating in his head. But this time the voice did not trail off so that he could nap. It kept buzzing in his mind. It kept him awake as he waited silently in the rain for his next and final turn, the turn that could crush forever all the hopes he had built up in himself, his family, his friends along the tortuous trail he had covered so swiftly to get to this folding chair on the soggy infield at the greatest athletic spectacle on earth.

Then he remembered the sign at the eastern end of the stadium, high above the stand on which the Olympic flame burned in its concrete bowl. The flame had been relayed by more than 1,500 runners, by plane and by ship, through seven countries, from Greece, where the first Games were held, to England. It was a symbol of friendship and cooperation between nations, voiced in the words on the sign by Baron de Coubertin, the Frenchman who had revived the modern festival.

He popped his head out of the blanket and looked at the sign above the rim of the stadium. Even through the rain the white letters stood out boldly:

"The important thing in the Olympic Games is not winning but taking part. The essential thing in life is not conquering but fighting well."

"Yes, it's not the winning," he told himself, "it's doing your best. And if I do my best that's all anyone can ask." His spirits lifted and as he bent his head down on his knees again there came to his mind a moment from the past. He was at another field; again he was high jumping, again the bar seemed out of reach. But he was even smaller then and he had screwed up his courage to try and he had made it—yes, his first high jump, back there on the playground with Gene and Bill Walker.

The small voice within him was still buzzing, but hadn't it changed its tune? What was it saying now? Not "don't worry," "don't worry," but "forget form, forget

68

form." As his name was called for his final attempt he kept thinking of that first jump way back in Tulare. How had he done it then? Yes, that was the way. He would do the same now.

This time he lined up more directly in front of the bar. For a second he looked up at the stands in the general direction of his folks. He studied the bar again. If he were standing by it, it would fit under his chin. Remember? He smiled inwardly. Then he was off. With all his might he ran, and with all his strength he exploded off the ground. Everyone watching him gaped. They had never seen such form before—if it could be called form. It looked strictly like heart, but it carried Bob over the bar.

Still thinking of that first jump as he picked himself up from the pit, he was on the brink of apologizing for —"for what?" the small voice said and then it was gone. His mind was clear and he was still in the running. He knew he would be all right after that.

Watching the drama had been Brutus Hamilton, an observer for the University of California, and Dink Templeton, veteran track authority. As Mathias dove over the bar Hamilton, usually undemonstrative, slapped Templeton on the back and cried: "The kid's going to win it!"

Smiling, Templeton said: "Yes, Brutus, I think that's the turning point. When you've been watching kids as long as you and I, you can spot a great one the instant you see him. Mathias has got it. He's the kind all coaches pray for and seldom find. There are plenty of good ones, but this one's a competitive genius."

69

Bob negotiated the next height on his first jump and he worked his way up to 6 feet, 1¼ inches, the highest he had ever gone. That tied Heinrich's best, and as Kistenmacher could do only 5 feet, 7 inches, the Frenchman took over first place in the point standings. Simmons, who had also tied for first, slipped by the Argentinian into second place, while Bob held third. Mondschein had fallen down at his specialty, barely clearing 6 feet. The high jump had been an ordeal, but after it Mathias gained confidence.

By the time the day's final test, the 400-meter run came around it was eight o'clock in the evening, but still light. Bob had been on the field ten hours. He was dead tired and he had had nothing to eat but sandwiches from a box lunch. But he still had enough left in him to show his heels to the rest of the runners in his heat and chalk up the respectable time of 51.7 seconds.

Kistenmacher came back to record the fastest time, 50.5 seconds, and Heinrich was close behind with 51.5; and these two finished the day in first and second place in that order. But as he walked off the track Mathias was stubbornly entrenched in third place with 3,848 points, only thirty-two behind Heinrich and forty-nine behind Kistenmacher.

Bob had time for only a brief reunion with his family before returning to Uxbridge. Just to reassure his mother he had told her he wouldn't lose. At this point, with Kistenmacher ahead, it was a little white lie.

After his exhausting day his stomach roared with hunger, he was tired and he wanted to get to bed early to regain as much strength as he could. Despite the bad weather and bad breaks he had surprised everyone by hanging on among the leaders. But he hoped for an even better day in the morning.

On the bus back to camp Bob cat-napped. When he got there, he crammed down his meal and immediately fell into a deep sleep.

He was up again at seven the next morning, but when he looked out of the window he saw that it was raining even harder than the day before. Again he had orange juice and steak, and again he rode the bus to the stadium to dress and warm up. His best events were coming up, but this downpour was slowing the track and would make treacherous going in the weights and pole vault. Also, as soon as he began limbering up he knew that his muscles were pretty sore and he wondered how they would respond when he asked them to carry him over the barriers in the day's opener, the 110-meter high hurdles.

Once inside the stadium Bob saw that again, in spite of the miserable weather, his family were by no means the only diehard enthusiasts present. The place was jammed with more than 60,000 spectators, protecting themselves with all sorts of raincoats, overshoes, galoshes, umbrellas, oilskins, blankets, and even newspapers.

Before the hurdles race began, Kistenmacher, who must have fancied himself an amateur psychologist, came over to Mathias and, thinking he would discourage the "baby" of the competition, told him: "Mathematically, I have it figured out that you can't beat me."

Bob didn't get rattled. He just looked blank and said

71

nothing. He wasn't too good at mathematics. He would have to see for himself.

As soon as the gun cracked, Bob knew he was in difficulty. The soreness in his legs was preventing him from jumping high enough and he grazed the first hurdle. When he came down he lost his balance and considerable momentum as well. He looked wobbly. He kept thinking that he was going to hit one of the hurdles for sure. But he kept going and managed to stay on his feet. Though he told a teammate that it was one of the worst hurdle races he had ever run, the time of 15.7 seconds was good, considering the conditions.

Instead of the pressure telling on Mathias, it cracked Kistenmacher, who stumbled on the last hurdle of his heat and dropped out of the first three in the point standings. Simmons, whose time of 15.2 seconds was the best of the lot, shot into first place. Heinrich held second and Mathias third. Bob didn't gloat over the Argentinian's misfortune. He had a forgiving nature and the way things were going he knew that it could have just as easily happened to him. The wet going had narrowed the field to thirty as five more contestants dropped out when the discus event got under way.

The discus was Bob's old love and on his first toss he threw it more than 145 feet, ahead of everyone else. Bob felt better. If that throw stood up, he would gain on the whole field. Then Mondschein stepped into the ring, went through his windup and threw the dish. It hit short of Mathias' previous effort, but slithered along the damp grass and knocked over Bob's marker.

The rain-coated officials went out to look for the hole

in which Mathias' indicator had been, but they couldn't locate it. Mondschein and Mathias joined the hunt, but couldn't find the hole either. After a half hour's search the officials gave up and placed a new marker for Mathias' toss obviously far short of his previous one. It now was at 144 feet, 4 inches.

When he saw what was happening Gene Mathias came rushing down to the field and called Bob. "Bob, why don't you make them look for it until they find it?" he fumed.

Bob pursed his lips and shook his head. "I can't hold everybody up. I guess my breaks are just going to stay bad."

"But Bob, if they set you back a foot you could lose enough points to shut you out of the first three places in a close thing like this," Gene said.

"I'm afraid there's nothing to be done," Bob answered.

Sure enough, on his next two throws he could not surpass his first one. As it turned out, however, neither could anyone else; the wet discus proved too difficult to grasp. It slipped completely out of Simmons' hand and the furthest the temporary pace setter could twirl it was 107 feet. He plunged from first place to fourth and when all the points were totaled, the name of Mathias went to the head of the list for the first time. He had 5,500 points to 5,452 for Heinrich.

When the discus measuring ended it was noon, and the rain began to come down in sheets. Thousands of fans began filing out and the others retreated to the cover of the roofed section which extended two-thirds of the way down the grandstand.

As Bob was leaving the field to get some sandwiches, an official stopped him. "Better not go," he warned. "The pole vaulting is starting and you're liable to be called any moment now." So Bob went back, wrapped himself in a blanket to keep warm and tried to get some rest.

Because they thought it would speed things up, the officials now divided the remaining athletes into two groups. Bob was put in the second group; thus he would have to sit by a longer time before he could start vaulting. He waited and waited and hunger gnawed at his body, but he felt that he could not leave the field for fear that he would be summoned for his first try.

In the gathering twilight the scene had become grotesque. On the field the athletes and officials were going painfully through their motions like phantoms in some improbable mystery. The stadium was rapidly emptying, except for a few thousand hardy souls, such as the Mathias family, remaining under the shelter of the grandstand roof. Between announcements the loud-speaker played dreamy music, "Over the Waves" and "The Merry Widow Waltz."

Finally, in the late afternoon, Mathias' group was instructed to begin pole vaulting. In the interval he had waited he would have had time to digest a six-course dinner, but now, like many others, he was forced to exert himself on an empty stomach.

Knowing that he would have to conserve every ounce of energy in his weakened condition, Bob turned down his chance at the beginning height of 8 feet, 6 inches.

When Gene saw his brother confer with the knot of officials and then walk away from the runway he became worried and again hurried down to the field.

"What's the matter, Bob?" Gene asked.

"The bar's too low. I'm waiting till it gets to ten feet."

Noticing other entrants sliding on the slippery runway and even slipping off the pole, Gene pleaded with his brother. "Look at the other guys. You're not too hot at this, Bob. If you make this height you'll at least get some points. But if you wait until later and then miss you won't get anything and it'll cost you your lead."

Bob refused to budge. "No, Gene, I've got to save myself. I'm not trying it until it gets to ten feet. I know I can do it."

Gene saw it was useless to argue and headed back up to his seat in the stands. "Stubborn so-and-so," he muttered. The event continued to drag and the vaulters continued to fumble around in the murk.

It was evening by the time the bar got to 10 feet and Bob entered the competition. By now it was so dark a white tennis shoe had been placed to mark the box in which the pole was placed for leverage, and a white handkerchief was tied to the crossbar. The stadium lights were turned on but they were only feeble fifty-watt bulbs and they hindered more than helped by casting confusing shadows on the field.

His family watched tensely as Bob poised for his takeoff at the head of the runway. Failure to clear 10 feet would nullify the entire bitter struggle he had waged to take the lead in the points race. Then Bob was churning down the sloppy strip, picking up speed.

He dug his pole in, sprang skyward and dropped neatly over the bar. His strength-saving gamble had paid off.

Time dragged on and still the vaulters kept climbing, their bodies drenched, their uniforms splattered with mud. Night had fallen and only a handful of people remained to watch the eerie proceedings As Bob awaited his turn again, the first group of decathlon men were finishing their final event, the 1500 meter run. Then one of the contestants slipped and collapsed on the track near Bob. Without hesitation, Bob ran over to the fallen figure, picked him up and walked him slowly around the track until he had recovered sufficiently to continue under his own power. Then Bob trotted back to the pole vault pit. By now the bar was at 11 feet. It was dangerous to go on. A misplaced pole could mean a serious accident like a broken arm or leg.

When the final results among the first group were posted, they showed that Heinrich of France with 6,974 points was slightly ahead of Simmons with 6,950. Simmons had edged past Kistenmacher, but now the burden of winning for Uncle Sam had fallen entirely on the shoulders of Mathias. Mondschein was in the second group, too, but Mathias was the only one who had a practical chance of overtaking the Frenchman. However, as he was weak in the metric mile, Mathias knew he had to pile up as many points as possible before he got to it in order to have a chance of winning.

So he kept at the pole vault until he had cleared 11 feet, 5¾ inches. He took two cracks at the next height, 11-9, but missed both. A small gang of students from George Pepperdine College in Los Angeles gathered

76

near the pit, yelling: "Come on, Tulare! Come on, Tulare!" Nevertheless Bob quit then, rather than risk a crippling injury.

With two events to go Bob trailed Heinrich by 786 points. He was dog tired, and to try to match the Frenchman's performance in the distance race, the closing activity, would be beyond his powers. There was no alternative to putting everything he had left into the javelin throw and drawing close enough so that a poor 1500 meters time would still put him ahead of Heinrich.

At ten o'clock that night the sky was black and the night stormy. The Olympic torch flickered defiantly against the wind at one end of the hushed stadium. Yet the light from it and the string of pale bulbs was insufficient to illuminate the field and the officials had to break out flashlights to enable the athletes to measure their run and see the foul line for the javelin toss. What had begun as merely a trial of athletic skill and physical endurance had now become a raw test of moral courage and psychological stability. A small group of newsmen and brave spectators hung on. Mrs. Mathias paced nervously in the stands. Dr. Mathias stood stoically by. Gene and little Jimmy fretted.

On his first throw Bob fouled. His family and the other Americans staying on groaned. Bob draped himself in his blanket and tried to keep his arm warm. Then he was called again. This time he watched his step more carefully, and as he came to the end of his run he threw all his remaining resources of purpose, knowledge and strength behind the spear. It disappeared into the gloom. Because they could not follow its flight the officials stood well to the side until it landed. Then they ran out to measure it. It was announced as 165 feet, good for 593 points. That brought Mathias up to within less than 200 points of Heinrich. If he could only run the 1500 meter in less than six minutes, he was in.

Dr. Mathias assured his wife: "Robert has only to stay on his feet to win." But Bob was so weary and sore and hungry by now, it was still doubtful he could do it. Gene rushed back to the field again to time Bob so that he would know how he was doing on each of the four laps.

As the runners lined up on the far side of the track all the Mathiases could see of the start of the race was the orange flash of the gun in the dark.

Presently some faint white blotches emerged from the darkness, around the first turn—the uniforms of the runners. As they passed by, the wavering light reflected them weirdly in the water-logged red brick track. Bob was far back, hopelessly outdistanced. But he was fighting only one enemy now—time. Then the ghostly figures merged with the blackness again at the far turn.

It seemed an eternity as Bob plodded around the track, cramps in his stomach and in one foot, and his elbow stinging from his recent effort of the javelin. Viewed through the rain, the pumping of his arms and legs resembled the leaden groping of swimmers at the bottom of a tank.

But it was only minutes. The big question was, how many?

As he neared the completion of the last lap most of the other athletes had already left the stadium. Heading into the back stretch, he leaned forward and Gene, waiting at the finish line, stop watch in hand, feared he was going to stagger and fall. Instead, Bob gritted his teeth and started to sprint. As he crossed the finish line and wobbled over toward his parents in the stands, the officials shone their flashlights on their stop watches for the verdict: 5 minutes, 11 seconds. He had done it. It was good for only 354 points, but it was enough to ensure victory.

In the arms of his mother, he gasped: "Are you happy, Mom?"

She hugged him and wept. "Never again, son, it's too hard."

Dr. Mathias, Gene and Jimmy stood by, grinning broadly. It was 10:35, more than twelve hours since Bob had started competing. Never had a decathlon been contested under more wretched conditions and never had anyone less than five years older than Bob conquered in the Olympics.

Bob padded barefoot into the dressing room and sank wearily on a bench. He was besieged by reporters and well-wishers and he summoned all of his patience to bear up under the usual barrage of questions.

"What are you going to do to celebrate, Bob?" a reporter asked.

Bob looked at him a moment. "Start shaving, I guess." The assemblage laughed.

"What made you keep going?"

"My Mom," Bob said. "All the way from Tulare she'd been telling everybody how worried she was. Mother thought I was just a little boy among men. I just had to show her she was wrong."

"Have you ever tried anything tougher?"

Bob shook his head. "I've never worked harder or longer in my life."

"Will you defend your title in 1952?" the same voice asked.

"I wouldn't do this again for a million dollars."

He had almost squirmed out of his track clothes before the crowd finally realized he deserved a respite and began breaking up. He showered and dressed and met his family outside. He turned down the proposal to go somewhere for a quiet celebration. "No, really, I'm too tired," Bob begged off. "Just go back to the hotel. I'll go to sleep and I'll see you tomorrow."

So, in the company of two teammates, Bob boarded a bus for Uxbridge. When he got there he went straight to bed. He still was deep in a drugged sleep when his roommates rousted him out at ten o'clock the next morning. "Come on, Bob," they yelled, "you'll miss the victory ceremony."

Telegrams had begun to arrive from all over the world. Bob took time to read a few, of which one was from President Harry S. Truman: "By winning the Olympic decathlon championship," it read, "you have demonstrated abundantly that the glory of America is its Youth. In the name of the nation to which you have brought such an outstanding distinction I extend hearty congratulations. All of your fellow Americans are proud of you."

What happened subsequently greatly influenced Mathias to reconsider his statement of the night before that he would never again try the decathlon.

Better weather had lured another packed house to the stadium. Then the official medal presentation for the decathlon was announced and, as the name "Mathias" hung on the air, the throng of 70,000 stood and strained for a look at the unbelievable teen-ager who had swept unheralded out of far-off California such a short time ago and had survived the grimmest ordeal in the history of the modern games to vanquish the flower of the world's iron-man athletes.

Even after his long night's rest Bob looked peaked as he mounted the podium, flanked by Heinrich and Simmons. It was no wonder. He had lost fifteen pounds in the two days of exertion. It was worth it, though. As he clutched his gold medal and heard the acclaim of the crowd and the band strike up its salute, he knew what a fine thing he had done for his family, his friends, and his country.

He glowed inside. All the hard, lonely hours of practice, the self-denial in diet, the strict personal habits, the heart tugs and bad breaks were worth this one brief instant.

Later, to friends, Mrs. Mathias, who was watching from the stands in a plain blue suit, surrounded by the radiant faces of her husband and her two other sons, described the thrill of that moment:

"When my child stood out there with those thousands of people at attention, and they raised the flag and the massed bands played The Star Spangled Banner just for him, I thought my heart would burst."

The United States won many medals at London and far outstripped all of the other countries in the unofficial team standings, but no victory was more gratifying to it than that of the modest youngster. News of his valiant deed was published around the world, and throughout the United States it was hailed in editorials.

Probably the *Idaho Daily Statesman,* of Boise, put it best when it wrote in its issue of August 9, 1948:

> We think the most notable Olympic victory . . . by any of Uncle Sam's athletes competing in the classic games was that of Bob Mathias, the seventeen-year-old California school boy who won the decathlon against the thirty-seven best all-around athletes in the world.
>
> While the American squad has won twenty-six gold medals, symbolic of first place in an Olympic event, in the games so far, and while the United States team . . . was far ahead of all other competing nations in team totals, there has prevailed a general attitude of 'what else can you expect, the Americans have hordes of entrants all over the place, they're bound to win more events than anyone else.'
>
> Young Mathias' victory, we think, takes the edge off that sort of deprecation. In the most exhaustive and conclusive test of athletic condition and skill, the decathlon, the California youth met the best the world had to offer in individual competition and beat them. . . . Man against man, he proved himself the best.
>
> Truly, he is the Olympic champion of champions and the United States need apologize to no other nation in proudly congratulating him on his remarkable victory.

Later that year, at a banquet in Los Angeles at which Mathias was feted, Paul Helms, Southern California sportsman and founder of the Helms Athletic Foundation, spoke for every bleacher in the land when he said: "We sent a boy over to do a man's job and he did it far better than any man ever could."

Chapter 6

HOMECOMING

SELDOM HAS A TOWN SO SPONTANEOUSLY DRAINED ITS heart of emotion as Tulare did when it heard that its hero, Bob Mathias, had prevailed in the Olympics.

Again, as after Mathias' triumph in the national decathlon championships at Bloomfield, the town's first warning was the ringing of the "scoop" bell on the teletype machine in the offices of the *Tulare Advance Register*. The electric impulses which typed out the story seemed to flow right out into the streets, and within minutes the town was crackling with excitement.

The tension had increased steadily that morning of August 6 when Bob, six thousand miles away, was deep in the decisive phase of his struggle. Many citizens, like Bob's grandmother, Mrs. Martha Harris, at her home at 251 North N Street, constantly monitored their radios for progress reports. Even before 9 A.M. the atmosphere in the Elks Club was jittery with anticipation. The Rotary Club, of which Dr. Mathias is a past president, broke into its regular luncheon program with bulletins.

As the day wore on it became harder and harder for people to pay attention to other matters. Like so many others, John Seavers, who was working in the Tulare High office, simply gave up and headed downtown in the early afternoon, accompanied by Coach Virgil Jackson and most of the rest of the school staff. On the way they burst into the Tulare Fight Song.

When finally the announcement of Bob's victory came, the built-up tension let go with a boom. Factory whistles began blowing and did not let up for forty-five minutes. Firechief R. E. Rounsaville cut loose the station house siren, and the fire engines raced out to parade around the streets. Hundreds of honking autos began heading from the residential areas and the roundabout farms toward downtown. They formed an impromptu procession, led by a sedan driven by Jack Doherty with huge white letters splotched in paint on the sides proclaiming, "Mathias for President."

The parade clogged the main shopping section and U.S. Highway 99 for three hours. Citizens collared each other in the streets, exchanged backslaps, and shouted, "Bob won!" Stores closed down and neighbors rang doorbells to start celebration parties. Soon an extra edition of the *Tulare Advance Register* was on the streets, with the biggest headline Editor Tom R. Hennion had ever run in peace or war. "Mathias Wins Olympic Title," it screamed in 114-point boldface type.

Back at her home Bob's grandmother wept tears of joy. "I'm just crying for happiness," she said, applying a handkerchief to her face. Then, thinking her sobbing might be misconstrued as lack of faith in Bob, she quickly added: "But I was expecting it. I knew he was good."

Bob's uncle, Marion Harris, who ran a Tulare nursery, put into words what most of the townsfolk had suffered through. "What I've been through today makes your hair stand up. These track meets are an old story, but today was different. I didn't know how he would do with that stiff competition and all those fellows against him. And he's just a kid who grew up under my feet.

"I felt sure after the seventh event the percentages were for him to win. I wasn't discouraged when he was reported tiring in the eighth event. He recuperates fast."

"I knew he could do it," Coach Ernie Lambrecht, who had tutored Bob in the hurdles, put in. "I was a little worried for a while, it was such a long wait. He was a wonderful athlete in high school. He has a good competitive spirit and he sure has the will to win and a wonderful family behind him. I was waiting for the final word and I thought: 'Isn't this ever going to get over with?'"

At the Chamber of Commerce, Secretary Harry Perry and his wife said, "We're just too thrilled to talk."

The local Western Union office had more telephone requests to wire congratulations to Bob than it could handle. Finally, growing impatient with the continuous busy signal, many people simply replaced their receivers and rushed to the office in person to compose their messages. It was late in the evening before the office could close.

Enthusiastic as was the response, it was as nothing

compared to what Tulareans promised they would do when Bob himself came home; plans were immediately set into motion to stage an official civic blow-off for that occasion.

Meanwhile Dr. and Mrs. Mathias and Jimmy were on their way back, convoying the Olympic medal Bob had turned over to them for safekeeping, while he saw the sights and competed in track exhibitions in Paris, Belfast and Dublin. Gene stayed behind to accompany his brother.

Hardly had he stepped off the victory pedestal than Bob felt the full force of the nerve-wracking trial a celebrity must endure. He was continuously ambushed by autograph-hounds, sports fans young and old, newsmen and cameramen, both amateur and professional. Before he left London he went shopping and was recognized in the stores. He bought a $20 cashmere sweater, a $5 hat, which he refused to wear once he got back to the States, and two briar pipes for his Dad.

In Paris he met city officials and signed the Gold Book reserved for famous visitors. In an interview, using his high school French, he said just the things that please Frenchmen the most:

"I like French cooking. It is better than English food. I am very happy to visit your country.

"Paris is beautiful. I like its avenues, its trees, and its monuments. I cannot describe it. It is a wonderful sight.

"The French girls are pretty, but I like California girls too. Yes," he grinned, "even better. Especially one." He left off with a meaningful smile.

After taking part in one track meet, shopping some

more—he bought a bottle of perfume and a few notions —and shooting roll after roll of film, Bob left France and went to Ireland.

The Irish particularly loved him. He was showered with gifts of linen and sterling. He responded with good showings at both Belfast and Dublin, and when he won the discus event at the latter site the crowd broke into loud cheers.

Everywhere he went he impressed people with his politeness and made more friends. Whenever he gave an interview or had his picture taken he made it a point to say, "Thank you."

Finally his European appearances were over and Bob boarded the *S. S. America* at Cobh, Ireland, on August 20. He was assigned to share a lower deck room with seven other athletes.

Bob's delay in returning merely lengthened the fuse of the homecoming firecracker the Tulareans were fashioning and gave them more time to add to the charge.

After a week at sea the *S.S. America* nosed into New York harbor early on the morning of Friday, August 27. It got in so far ahead of time that a parade and official reception scheduled for the afternoon was canceled because most of the 168 athletes aboard wanted to start their journeys home. But New York made up for that at the docks, according the boat the most noisy welcome since the first GI's returned from World War II.

Escorted by two police tugs in its short trip up the harbor, the vessel was forced to return the three-whistle salute of other ships thirty-one times. Two fireboats set up huge sprays, an orchestra played on the promenade deck, and 5,000 people yelled and waved from the pier.

Questioned by reporters as he landed, Bob said: "I've reconsidered and I might try the decathlon again in 1952 at Helsinki."

He was one of the few arrivals to pause briefly in New York because he wanted to visit the YMCA and Hi-Y national offices. On hand to greet him and present him with a national Hi-Y plaque for his work in that organization were George B. Corwin, national Hi-Y secretary, and other New York area members.

After that Red Strader, then football coach of the professional New York Yankees and another San Joaquin prep hero at Modesto, took charge of Bob and brother Gene and arranged for them to see a baseball doubleheader that afternoon between the Yankees and Cleveland.

That night Bob and Gene climbed aboard a United Airliner for the trip to the Coast. At 8:45 on the morning of August 28 the plane landed at San Francisco airport, and for the first time in weeks Bob was again on the soil of his beloved home state.

Leaning on a gnarled hawthorn shillelagh he had picked up in Ireland, he was interviewed briefly while he waited to change to a plane that would take him and Gene to Visalia, the air stop nearest Tulare.

"How are you standing up under all this travel?" one reporter asked.

Bob was pretty weary, but all he said at first was: "Sure is rough on the crease of a guy's trousers."

"Aren't you tired at all?"

"Yes, I'm still very tired."

"What do you want to do most right now, Bob?" he was asked.

"Get some rest," he said. Then recalling the string of celebrations he knew were being prepared in his honor, he added, "but it doesn't look like I'll be able to for a while."

Then it was 9:15 and time for him to get on a United Airliner local that would take him to Visalia. He and Gene were followed up the ramp by a group of reporters and radio men who were covering his homecoming. While still air bound he gave a fifteen minute radio interview.

Around 11:30 the plane made a short stop at Fresno and then took off again. Bob grew visibly more nervous. Prescott Sullivan, writer for the *San Francisco Examiner,* who had probably first referred to Mathias as the All-American boy, asked, "What's the matter, Bob? You look worried."

"Well, I just hope there isn't a big crowd there," Bob said. "Only a few—Mother and Dad, the family, and—" he blushed—"I was thinking of my girl friend."

About noon, as the plane circled over Plaza Field, Visalia, Bob peered out of the window and saw that, contrary to his wish, there was a big crowd on hand. He gulped. "Holy smoke! There must be a million people down there! This is worse than the decathlon. I hope they don't ask me to make a speech."

The throng was so near the runway that the pilot had to ask the tower to clear the field before he would attempt a landing. Bob groaned and buried his head in his hands.

Then he had to fasten his safety belt and before he could think of much else the plane had landed and was taxiing to a halt. As the stewardess opened the door, Bob shrugged: "Might as well face it. I can't see any way out."

The crowd of 5,000 had begun assembling at ten o'clock and had waited patiently in the 100 degree heat. Their cars dotted the field, waiting to join the motorcade that would escort Bob the nine miles from the airport to Tulare. They had been herded behind a rope some distance from the plane, but when they got a glimpse of Bob they broke through the rope and surged toward him.

Before he could take a step off the ramp Bob was grabbed by a knot of his former Tulare teammates and hoisted onto their shoulders. Newsreel men, standing on autos, ground away. Cameras clicked. Reporters fought to get near him. Radio men, trailing a tangle of wires, tried to lift a microphone up to his lips. But Bob belonged to the mob and only by its dispensation was he allowed to say a few words into the mike. "This is swell," he said and then he was being borne off again.

Finally he was set down near where his beaming parents stood, and a small circle was cleared around them, but before he could greet them he was again asked to pose for pictures. When the photographers released him, he shook hands heartily with his father,

92

then kissed his mother. She began to cry and said, "This is wonderful." His brother Jimmy pounded him on the back and said, "Hi, Bob. Nice goin'." Bob grabbed his sister Patricia and swung her to his shoulders.

When he let his sister down, Bob looked around hesitantly and the crowd, guessing his thoughts, pushed forward a pretty brunette, sixteen-year-old Beverly Nesbitt, whom Bob had been dating since the start of the year. "Kiss Beverly," a camera man shouted and the crowd echoed him. Bob obliged and both he and Beverly blushed as Mrs. Mathias quickly wiped the lipstick off her son's lips. Finally the crowd around them parted long enough to let Gene Mathias through to embrace the family, too.

Mrs. Mathias was alarmed at the way Gene looked. "You're so thin," she said.

"I missed your home cooking, Mom," Gene smiled.

"How much weight did you lose?"

"About twenty pounds, but it was the greatest five weeks of my life."

Dick Wegener, chairman of the welcoming committee, urged Bob toward the blue convertible waiting with its top down, fifty feet away to head the procession to town. But the crowd kept milling and it took Bob twenty minutes to move that distance and take his place atop the convertible, his feet on the rear seat. On the seat itself were his mother and father. In front with Wegener, who drove, were Eugene, Jimmy and Patricia, who sat on Gene's lap.

Under the leadership of Lyle Larrette, the Tulare High band, in which Bob had once played and which

93

had so often joyously tooted in the wake of one of his spine-shivering touchdown runs, broke again into "Hail, Hail Tulare." The crowd finally scattered to the waiting autos for the start of the motorcade.

Thirty state highway patrolmen blocked off U.S. 99 and with their sirens shrieking cleared the way for the parade. The blue convertible, with a picture of Mathias attached to its front end, smiling through the words, "Olympic Decathlon Champion" and "Welcome Home, Bob," swung onto the steaming highway. The other cars, honking their horns, strung out behind in a line more than a mile long.

As the motorcade sped through the cotton fields and vineyards of the big Tagus Ranch, workers paused to wave and cheer. A private plane overhead, belonging to Ed Rose, a Tulare businessman, gunned its motor as its special tribute to Bob. The blowing of the whistles from the nearby creameries and factories added to the din.

Near the town itself the spectators, estimated to number 10,000 along the entire route, grew thicker. The procession slowed down. The people lining the road clapped and cheered. Bob began recognizing some individuals, and waved to them, calling them by their first names. He leaned over to shout to his mother: "It's not so bad after all. At least they didn't ask me to make a speech."

All Tulare wore a festive air and along K Street, in the heart of town, the crowd, in their white shirts and light summer dresses, spilled three deep off the curb on each side. Because of the jam the cars had slowed to a crawl. The heat beat down but stayed no one's enthusiasm. Everyone had turned out—oldsters, mothers with babies in their arms, and the youngsters. Especially the youngsters. As soon as the parade had rolled into the city limits a drove of small fry on bikes had joined it, riding alongside Bob's car, grinning and shouting to the champ: "Hi, Bob! Nice goin', Bob!" They felt they had a special claim on him. To them he was a very personal hero. "Some day," each told himself: "I'm going to be where he is."

It was not so improbable. Not long ago Bob had been as small as they, playing on these very streets. And now he was a world hero, an Olympic titlist, but still a swell guy who did not forget his friends back home.

A huge sign, "Welcome Home, Bobby," was stretched across K Street, and bunting flew from the overhead wires. One theater had a "Welcome Home, Bob" sign topping its billing of Paulette Goddard and Roy Rogers. Many kids were blowing up special balloons made for the occasion, with "Congratulations" and "Welcome Home, Bob" printed on them. The stores were closed and most of them had welcome signs posted. Others had poses of Bob in various phases of the decathlon painted right on their windows by two talented state highway patrolmen, Dub Kramer and Les Conradi. The Elks Club had so many visitors it practically held open house.

At last the motorcade reached the city hall, where Mayor Elmo Zumwalt, a physician like Bob's dad, who had been prevented from going to the airport because he had had to deliver two babies, was waiting. He

95

vigorously shook Bob's hand and made a very short official welcoming speech. "We're all proud of you, Bob. The evidence of Tulare's feeling is in sight for everyone to see," he said. Then he gave Bob the keys to the city. The crowd roared its amen.

City Manager Tom Fennessy said: "Nothing so great or fine has ever happened to Tulare."

Among the official greeters on the city hall steps was Fred (Dad) Smith, veteran police judge, and when Bob stepped forward to wring his hand, tears came to the old man's eyes.

In a few words, Mathias revealed to the crowd his future plans. "I'm going to try to get some rest, but from what I understand I may not be able to. Then I'll go to Kiski Prep and later, I hope to Stanford."

The mob then realized that Bob was worn out and they let him go home, but he was far from through for the day. The press followed, as did some of Bob's closest friends, like Sim Iness, who had just missed making the Olympic team as a discus thrower. They wanted to get the story of his success from Bob's own lips and they crowded the living room of the Mathias home, plying Bob with questions about the long trial he underwent to capture the gold medal.

Patricia, the only Mathias who had not witnessed the triumph because she was on vacation in King's Canyon National Park with friends, had to tell her brother how she heard the news:

"A man from a radio station phoned me that you won the decathlon. So we all made paper signs with 'Bob Mathias, Olympic Champion' on them and had our own parade. We put paper streamers on the car, too. Later we drove to the ranger station and I asked the ranger if there was a telegram there for Miss Patricia Mathias. He said, 'no,' but I didn't care. I just wanted him to know who I was. Then I went to the store and bought a triple decker ice cream cone."

Bob roared and poked his sister and she giggled. The questions continued to fly. The cameramen asked Bob to step out into the backyard and he posed chinning himself. "Guess I'd better be getting ready for the next Olympics," he cracked.

When he went back into the house, Bob felt worn out and sleepy. He excused himself, went into the kitchen, drank a quart of milk and went upstairs to his bedroom. He locked the door, put on some phonograph records and lay on the bed, gradually dozing off. Downstairs the gathering slowly dispersed only because it knew that there would be another chance to blow off steam in the official town welcoming ceremony the following Monday night.

When the noise had subsided along K Street, one old-timer remarked: "This was louder than on V-J Day. It's the biggest thing we've ever had." The *Tulare Advance-Register* seconded him. It called the affair: "the biggest day in Tulare's 60-year history." A grizzled Tularean meditated: "It must have been something like this when Lindbergh came back to St. Louis."

A local jeweler, Manuel Toledo, returning to his store after the hoop-la found that the picture of Mathias pasted on his window had been partly torn off and

97

crushed, as though it had been embraced, and there were lipstick traces all over Bob's portrait.

The next day, Sunday, Bob lolled around the backyard, petting his dog, and answering more questions from the myriad kids who came to see their idol and from some of the newspapermen who called back. Noyes Alexander, sports editor of the *Tulare Advance-Register,* wanted to know about a movie offer Bob had received.

"What about this deal to play Tarzan, Bob?" Alexander queried. Another former decathlon champion, Glenn Morris, had starred as a jungle man after winning at the 1936 Berlin Olympics.

"Not this time," Bob said. "I'm going to school. Maybe in four years."

Then Bob Hoegh, a Tulare High chum who also was going to go to Kiski, dropped over. The pair went to a nearby playground and spent the rest of the afternoon throwing a football around.

The following night at the testimonial dinner eight hundred persons crowded the Tulare County Fairgrounds cafeteria for the banquet. There had been many more requests for tickets, but there was no more space. Later, six thousand onlookers overflowed the grandstand for the outdoor half of the program. Guests included Governor Warren and Morris, who still held the world's decathlon record of 7,900 points. He had come down from a Naval hospital in Oakland where he was recuperating from a World War II wound.

As the speeches heaped more and more praise upon him, Bob fidgeted. "The eyes of millions of boys are on

Bob Mathias," Governor Warren said, "not only for what he continues to do as an athlete, but for what he does as a citizen." Eyeing the Mathias boys, Gene, Bob and Jimmy, the Governor, who has three daughters, cracked, "I should have brought my family with me."

But it was Mrs. Mathias who put a lump in the throat of every parent present when she described her reactions while watching Bob at London.

"I looked down on that field where my little boy was and there were thirty-seven of the world's greatest athletes representing nineteen countries. I must confess I saw just one of them most of the time—our Robert.

"It seemed to me only seven years back I used to comb that boy's hair, wash his face, wipe his nose and make sure he would get away to school in time.

"And there he was, competing against the greatest athletes in the world and just a boy. You can believe me when I say it was one of the greatest things a mother could ever watch. Robert, a little boy to me, as he would be to any mother, was doing as well as the world had to offer—and better."

When Bob got up to speak, he was less nervous than Tulare had seen him during other public appearances, but he still was visibly affected. Clearing his throat, he said: "The biggest thrill in my life was when I stood on that victory stand in Wembley Stadium. But I will remember the parade you held for me and this banquet longer than anything else in my life." He paused and added shyly: 'Thanks for voting for the school bonds so that other kids can have the chance I had. I thank

99

you from the bottom of my heart." He was presented with a gold watch.

The following night in Fresno Bob had to endure another toast. Three thousand people gathered in Ratcliffe Stadium, where but a few months before Bob first got the "inside" on the decathlon from slightly skeptical older hands, and presented him with a trophy in the name of the people of Fresno. As happened so often in an affair involving Bob there were complications. A power failure shut off the lights in the stadium for twenty-five minutes, but cars at the field switched on their lights and the battery of one was used to power the mike so the ceremony could continue. The mayor of Fresno, Glenn M. De Vore, Congressman B. W. Gearhart, Glenn Morris, and others spoke.

Again Mrs. Mathias was eloquent. "I can't thank the people of a great city like Fresno enough for turning out like this for a little boy from Tulare. They have hung another great star in the sky for millions of youngsters to reach for in the future."

Morris captured the audience with his tribute. "When my decathlon record is broken I hope Bob will do it. I did not know Bob until yesterday, but I'll say it couldn't happen to a better fellow."

Athletes from Fresno State College performed the events of the decathlon and Morris commented: "I like your celebration for Bob better than the one I had. Here you have other athletes performing the various events in the decathlon. In Denver after I won they made me do it."

Two nights later Bob went to Los Angeles as guest of

the *Los Angeles Times* at a charity professional football game. He was introduced along with other Olympic Games winners and entrants. As his name was called 77,000 voices cried their appreciation.

From Los Angeles Bob flew to Sacramento with Gene to receive more honors at the California State Fair. The brothers took in the exhibits Friday afternoon and then Bob stopped in front of a weight guesser.

"You're twenty-four years old and you weigh 197 pounds," the man said. "I'm only seventeen," Bob grinned. When he stepped on the scale the pointer stopped at 193. Bob picked out a red plaster dog as his prize and later added a green one at another concession.

That night Bob was introduced before the grandstand, with 10,000 people in attendance. He was offered a seat down in front in the judges' section, where the Governor also sits when there. "No, thanks," Bob said. "I'd rather sit where I can see the whole show." And he took off for the bleachers, higher up.

When he got there and was confronted by a fifteen-year-old, Bob apologized, "Gee, I'm sorry, I don't have a ticket for this section."

"Gosh," the usher exclaimed, "You can have any seat you want in the house and I'll see that you get it."

The next day was "Bob Mathias and Tulare County Day." Bob went on the air twice and was honored at the annual press-radio luncheon of the fair. Tulare County won second place in the competition for the best display of processed agricultural and horticultural products.

But it was getting close to Bob's departure deadline and the Mathias family, which had driven up from Los Angeles after the football game, left with Mr. and Mrs. Albert O. Hoegh and their son Bob for San Francisco to put the two on the plane for Pennsylvania.

However, the effects of that brief but triumphant homecoming were to linger for a long time. It was noticed that for the first time so late in summer, youngsters flooded the high school track, practicing running, jumping and throwing the weights.

One Tularean, Harry Davis, who had been on the Bob Mathias reception committee, told Mrs. Mathias of how her son's return had stirred the imaginations of his youngster. "The other day my little boy said, 'Dad, I gotta have a football suit and helmet just like Bob Mathias.' So I went out and bought them. Bob has done wonders for this city and the kids. He's their hero.

One day an old man came to the Mathias residence and rang the doorbell. Mrs. Mathias answered.

"Pardon me, M'am," he said. "I just came by to pay my respects."

Mrs. Mathias invited him inside.

"Mrs. Mathias," the oldster said, "I've known for a long time that Bob was going to be a great leader of young boys."

Mrs. Mathias became more curious. "How?" she asked.

"It's foretold in the Bible," the old man said quietly. "I'll show you."

Mrs. Mathias handed him the copy of the New Testament Bob had taken with him to the Olympic Games.

The old man opened it to "The Acts" Chapter I, verse 26, and he read, in a voice quivering slightly from emotion: "And they gave forth their lots; and the lot fell upon Matthias; and he was numbered in the eleven Apostles."

The Number 11 has always been a lucky one for the Mathias family. Bob wore it all through high school, in football, basketball, and track. Quite by accident he was Number 11 of the Americans who competed in Scotland and Ireland in 1948. That same year, when Bob graduated from high school, the school retired the number and gave him all shirts, jackets and uniforms with 11 on them. Eugene also wore Number 11 during his high school career. Jimmy, however, couldn't get a Number 11 uniform to fit him; consequently he chose Number 33, since, as he said, he was the third son in the family. But he later got a Number 11 sweat suit, and so was 33 on the field and 11 on the bench. Mrs. Mathias says that the number has always been a charmed one for her sons.

Julius Friedman, courthouse reporter for the *Tulare Advance-Register,* told another journalist: "I'm not fooling about this—Bob Mathias' victory in the Olympic Games and his all-around fine sportsmanship in school here have done more to combat juvenile delinquency in Tulare than any other happening."

But probably the finest postscript to Bob's homecoming was a letter, written on Metro-Goldwyn-Mayer Pictures stationery, that arrived at the Mathias home shortly after the welcoming ceremonies. It read:

9826 BURGEN AVENUE
LOS ANGELES 34, CALIFORNIA
29 AUGUST 1948

My Dear Dr. and Mrs. Mathias:

This isn't an M-G-M letter; rather, an omnibus letter to convey to you two the impressions of all the veteran newsreel men who covered the return of Bob to his home town. I missed the pleasure of meeting you, although I saw you in the press at the airport. But the boys delegated to me the pleasant chore of writing on behalf of all: Joe Johnson of Universal; Col. Sam Greenwald of Paramount; Norman Alley of M-G-M's News of the Day; and Willard Vanderveer of Warner-Pathé. I fit into the picture only as former editor of Paramount News—ex-boss for three of the four.

You have our joint congratulations not only on Bob, but on your whole fine family. We are all of us fathers (and a couple of us grandfathers!) and before going to Tulare, we speculated on the effect of a world-spotlight on a 17-year-old American youngster; over the years, we have seen a few sad examples.

The demeanor of your lad gave us a lift; and that's the real reason for this letter. After the event, we agreed that here at least was one kid whose background armed him against glamour-fever; whose wise parents had provided him with a measuring stick so that he could understand the high evaporation point of headlines. On that score, most surely he is to be congratulated; for during the next five or ten years, it is more than likely he will have to take the glare of wide publicity . . .

Please extend for all the newsreel men our most sincere thanks to the celebration committee, in particular Messrs. Tyler and Davis; there were many others, including the fine youngsters who drove our cars; I would list them all if I could recall their names. . . .

It is not very often that I have seen veteran newsfilm men so impressed as were this group; with the overall feeling summing up to this: congratulations are due, of course, to Bob—but our top congratulations go to you two for all-American tops in a championship job of parentage.

With sincere respect,

(Signed) William C. Park,
COMMANDER, U.S.N.R. (Inac.)

Chapter 7

KISKI DAYS

THE REPORTER FROM THE WASHINGTON, D.C., NEWS was waiting outside the restaurant for his girl. When she finally showed up—late as usual—the reporter did not say anything except, "Hi, Ethel," and quickly hustled her inside. Ethel was so surprised at his mild reaction that she did not even say, "Hi, Joe." She just kept looking at him. Obviously he had something else on his mind.

After they had ordered and laid aside the menus, Joe let escape a little laugh and, staring off into the distance as though he were seeing again a past incident, said, "Ethel, I had the funniest interview today. Not really funny—unusual, I guess."

"What happened?" Ethel asked.

"This kid Bob Mathias came to town to—"

"Bob Mathias?" Ethel interrupted. "Who's he?"

Joe showed none of that disgust which usually crosses a man's face at a feminine display of ignorance about sports. He's really in a pretty good frame of mind, thought Ethel.

"Bob Mathias is the California schoolkid who only beat about thirty grown men in the decathlon—" Joe waved his hand to indicate that he saw another question coming. "The decathlon is a ten-event test at the Olympics of all sorts of running, jumping and throwing ability that drags over two days and decides the best all-around athlete in the world.

"Anyway, he's going to Kiski Prep near . . ."

"Kiski Prep?" echoed Ethel, wide-eyed.

Joe shut his eyes, turned his head aside momentarily, opened his eyes and rubbed the back of his neck with his hand, in an action that said, "Lord, give me strength." Then he set his mouth in a straight, determined line and explained in measured tones:

"That's Kiskiminetas Springs Preparatory School at Saltsburg, Pennsylvania, near Pittsburgh. It's one of those private schools, like Lawrenceville, Taft, Groton— you know, Roosevelt went to Groton.

"So anyway President Truman asked Mathias down to get acquainted and Tom Clark, the attorney general, went on the radio with him later in a nation-wide broadcast. Mathias had been picked by the Radio Sportscasters of America as the 'Youth of the Year.'

"After he got through we talked to him and, frankly, Ethel, I've been reporting for five years and I've never seen a more modest, candid, friendly guy.

"When we asked him questions he would sort of stand there with a few wisps of his brown hair sticking stiffly out over his forehead, plunge his hands into his pockets, chew his gum real fast, rock on his heels, and bend over to make sure that he got the question right.

Then a sort of puzzled look would come over his face, as if to say, 'What's so remarkable about that?' And he only beat thirty of the best athletes in the world in two days of miserable weather and in the toughest kind of competition. Heaps of words have been written about him and it no more affects him than rain on a duck's back. Then he would shrug his shoulders and search his mind for details of his childhood or sports record and he tried his best to answer everything we asked.

"He was always polite and answered quietly and he was very frank, not phoney. We asked him, 'How do you like being a celebrity?' and he said, 'Fine, you get to meet such interesting people.' And, like Sam Stavisky of the *Post* said, he's got that refreshingly normal, healthy, happy look, as though any minute he's gonna bust out and ask, 'When do we eat?'"

Joe grew more thoughtful. Then he continued, "You know, Ethel, after you've been a newshound a while you get a little bitter. You see so much corruption and cynicism you begin to think it's typical and that the country is going plumb to the devil.

"Then out of nowhere a fresh breeze like this Mathias blows in, and when you get a whiff of the wholesomeness of a guy like that it makes you realize that the country is still pretty sound and powerful. It was a real pick-up, believe me. Oh, there's the waitress."

The Bob Mathias legend was snowballing. From all over the world fan letters poured into his Tulare home. Mathiases in Czechoslovakia, England, France, Germany wanted to know if they were in any way related

109

to Bob. His high school coaches were besieged with inquiries on how they trained such a marvel. His comings and goings continued to flush camera bugs and autograph collectors. And all over the land small boys, seeing his picture and reading of his heroism, resolved to model their lives after his.

Bob seemed just too good to be true and, in the minds of many who did not know him or had not seen him, doubt lingered as to his real capabilities. This reluctance to accord Mathias his due caused a flareup among Tulare writers and fans when Bob first entered Kiski and turned out for the football squad.

Misunderstanding exists about the reason Bob went to Kiski, and about the real purpose of the school. Many still believe Bob went there because he wanted to enter Stanford eventually and Kiski was a proving ground for future Indian athletes.

Many Stanford sports greats, such as Alf Brandin, the present business manager at the University, Bones Hamilton, Billy Laird, Monk Moscrip, and Horse Reynolds had prepped at Kiski, but actually Bob enrolled strictly for scholastic reasons.

As early as March of 1948, long before he had thought seriously of the decathlon or become tagged as the "greatest all-around athlete of all time," Bob had filled out an application form for the Pennsylvania school. Desiring to study medicine at Stanford, Bob had to make up high school deficiencies in English and mathematics. A friend of Gene Mathias, Bob Scott of Fresno, who had gone to Kiski and had no athletic reputation, recommended his school to the family.

Dr. Mathias investigated and found that Kiski had an excellent reputation for teaching, building character, and developing leadership. More of its graduates became preachers than football players. The entire student body attends church every morning.

After the relative freedom and informality of his home town high school, Bob found the confinement of the prep school campus a little terrifying. He had learned from the rigors and self-sacrifice of his training periods, however, that happiness and success come most readily from a well-ordered life. He quickly adjusted to the new routine.

The ivy-covered English style buildings of the school were full of tradition and memories of graduates who had spread Kiski's fame into the larger world of college athletics. Since its founding in 1888 by a grandfather of its present football coach, Jim Marks, Jr., the school had graduated more than seventy All-American and All-Sectional football players, and numerous other sports stars. Among them were Jim Davies, Jim DeHart, and Herb Stein of the famous 1916 Pittsburgh eleven. So were Harry Stuhldreher, one of the Four Horsemen of Notre Dame; Jim Daniels of Ohio State; and Cliff Montgomery of Columbia.

The classes at Kiski were small, only ten boys. To each ten was assigned one teacher, who taught only one subject. The classes studied one subject at a time for a nine week period, until each of the students had stuck with the subject long enough to become really interested in it as well as proficient.

The school day was divided into three periods. From

111

8:30 in the morning to 3:30 in the afternoon there were classes, each preceded by a supervised study hour. From 3:30 to 5 in the afternoon every boy took part in some form of athletics. In the evenings there were activities of various kinds for those boys whose marks were high enough for them to be excused from another supervised study period. Bob's marks were soon averaging between eighty-five and ninety.

The old boys at Kiski had received Bob with caution, making clear to him that they weren't scared by his press clippings and trophies. Presently his easy sense of humor won them over. He joined the glee club, and in his free time delighted his schoolmates with the cowboy numbers he sang while he strummed his guitar.

His room in Powers Hall contained his trophies, but the most prominent place in it was reserved for photographs of his Olympic teammates. Two months after school began, his classmates gave him a surprise party to celebrate his eighteenth birthday.

Of the school's enrollment of 174, fully one hundred boys turned out for football. Often they were scions of athletically famous families—Harry Stuhldreher, Jr. and William Sutherland, nephew of the late Jock Sutherland, who kept Pitt in the gridiron limelight for so long.

Possibly it was because so much talent had passed through Kiski that coach Jimmy Marks, Jr. underrated Mathias when he greeted the football squad for its first practice.

Previous performances and press clippings meant little to Marks. Every boy had to prove himself. That suited Mathias fine. He was very reticent about his for-

112

mer doings and his schoolmates really had to draw him out to make him talk. "I wish everybody would forget I won the decathlon," Bob told one of them.

But Marks' statements and actions began to cause a lot of doubt, especially in a certain California town, about his qualifications as a judge of athletic skill.

In one of the early practice sessions Marks asked Bob if he would like to be switched from the backfield to the line. "You see, Bob, I've got two lettermen fullbacks on hand from last year," Marks pointed out. "Wouldn't you like to try tackle or end?"

"If it's all the same with you, Mister Marks," Bob answered quietly, "I'd like to stick to fullback."

"I can't guarantee you'll make first string," Marks warned.

"I never asked for any guarantees, Mister Marks," Bob said, eyeing him steadily. "I'll just take my chances along with the rest of the fellows."

To the press, Marks reiterated his doubts about Mathias making good at the fullback slot. "He's certainly a fine boy and just about as willing a worker as I have on the squad," the coach told reporters. "He wants to play fullback, but I'm not sure he will make first string. I have a couple of good fullbacks back from last year who may beat him out.

"He has tremendous speed once he is underway, but he is a bit slow on the start. He may prove to be a great line backer. We will have to wait for a few scrimmages to see. I would like to see him up front as a tackle or end, but I have not been able to convince him he should make the change."

When that story got on the wires and filtered out to Tulare, the town blew its top.

Bob Sheley, a columnist for the now-defunct *Tulare Bee*, immediately took up the challenge. He blistered: "Unless the type of boys who attend eastern prep schools has changed drastically in recent years, Kiski is hardly so overburdened with athletic talent that Bob can't make the first team. There are plenty of senior colleges that don't have more than a handful of men the size of Bob.

"As for his ability, that needs no discussion or defense. It is well-known around the San Joaquin Valley.

"Maybe Bob won't make Kiski's first team. Perhaps Bob Hoegh won't either.

"However, up here on the coast at Palo Alto there is a small school called Stanford. Head Coach Marchie Schwartz, a better than fair player himself at a little midwestern college known as Notre Dame, is wishing the two Bobs were on the campus right now. Both probably will be there in 1949 but he'd feel better if they already had arrived."

That set the stage for Bob to decide the issue by his exploits on the gridiron. And that's just the way Bob wanted it. He always was better at action than at words.

One of the first things Bob did in practice was to injure his hand. But that didn't stop him. He kept battling for the first string fullback job. Before the lineup was picked for Kiski's opening game, however, Mathias was called to Washington to meet the President and the Attorney General in connection with the youth program sponsored by the latter.

114

Bob flew in accompanied by Kiski's headmaster, Dr. L. M. Clark. The California husky was wearing a loud checkered sports coat, a fiery, hand-painted tie and slacks. On the trip he planned to buy himself a couple or more pairs of pants because he had taken off in such a hurry from school that he had forgotten to bring an extra pair.

As soon as he arrived at the airport he was caught up in a whirlwind of activity. He was met at the field by Arthur Cook, a baby-faced local lad who had won an Olympic medal for rifle marksmanship and was also being feted along with Mathias. Though twenty years old, Cook stood only five feet, six inches, and weighed only 120 pounds. Cook was a student at the University of Maryland, but alongside Mathias it was he who looked like the prepster and Bob like a college man.

The two were whisked in a special car to the White House, where they shook hands with President Truman, who took them on a personally conducted tour of the Chief Executive's quarters. They talked about the Olympics and the President told them that he and the country were proud of them.

Later at a press conference President Truman repeated his remarks. "In my opinion this is what makes the country great—to produce such men as these, who go out and make a name for themselves. It is good not only for them but good for the country and for the world. I hope they will continue to be good citizens and will themselves have sons who will win an Olympic Gold Medal."

When the President was finished, a reporter queried Bob, "What are you doing now at Kiski?"

"Playing a little football," Bob said. "I'm out for fullback."

"Do you think you'll make first string?"

Bob looked puzzled for a moment, then said, "Why not?" At least he had confidence in his own ability.

"What track event do you like the most?" someone else asked.

"The discus," Bob smiled. "It's easiest."

Before they left the White House the President reached over to his desk and handed Bob a pencil. When he got outside he noticed that it had printed on it, "I swiped this from Harry Truman."

After lunch with Tom Clark at his private dining room in the Department of Justice, Mathias and Cook joined the Attorney General later that night on a radio broadcast to the nation's youth.

Clark gave Bob a combination wrist and stop watch inscribed, "Bob Mathias, Youth of the Year." It was presented by the Theater Owners of America, who had taken the lead in observing September as "Youth Month," following President Truman's proclamation.

In accepting the award, Bob told the listening audience the key to his background. "Our slogan always has been, 'a family that plays together stays together,' and it has worked fine for us."

Late that night Bob and Dr. Clark flew back to Kiski. On the plane Bob remembered that he had not bought the pants as he had intended. "Oh, well, I'll do it next time I get to a big city," he told Dr. Clark, and fell asleep.

Back at school, Mathias turned his attention again to his books and the torrid three-cornered contest for the starting fullback position. The season opener was almost at hand and Coach Marks would imminently announce the first string. Bob threw everything he had into every block, tackle and run. His hard work repaid him and when Coach Marks posted the list of eleven regulars Mathias was at fullback and Hoegh at end, just as their hometown supporters knew they would be.

The first game was against Indiana (Pennsylvania) State Teachers College reserves. After a tough battle, Harry Stuhldreher, Jr., Bob's roommate, intercepted a pass in the fourth quarter and lugged it back into scoring position on the visitors' 15-yard line. Kiski drove to the one, where the ball was fed to Mathias, who rammed the line for the touchdown. The final score was 7-0.

It was shortly after that first game that President Truman arrived in Tulare on his now-famous whistle stop tour that turned the tide in the presidential election of 1948. Four thousand people gathered around the Presidential special as it drew up to a siding. The President, appearing on the back platform, declared: "The San Joaquin Valley not only raises wonderful crops but also mighty fine people. And that includes Bob Mathias, who was in to see me the other day." The throng cheered.

"Bob is typical of the new generation of Americans," Truman continued, "who are brought up in a wholesome home life—a life which will contribute to the peace of the world."

In a way, one of the local newspapers predicted the election result not only in California but in the nation at large on the basis of the candidates' acquaintance with Tulare's best-known citizen.

Editorializing on the appearance of both Truman and Tom Dewey in Tulare, the *Tulare Bee* wrote: "We have no doubt that Dewey, like Earl Warren and Harry Truman, would admire and remember Bob, had he the chance to meet the champ. On this score, Tom will pass through Tulare at a disadvantage with Harry, who already knows about Bob."

Meanwhile Bob's gridiron prowess was increasing and despite his definite leaning toward Stanford, alumni of many other universities continued to pursue him.

In its next outing Kiski ground down the Washington and Jefferson freshmen, 32-0. Mathias didn't score, but his long punts kept the losers pinned in their own territory. About this time he was informed that the Pacific Association of the Amateur Athletic Union had nominated him as its candidate for the James E. Sullivan Memorial Award, given annually to the amateur who does most to advance the cause of sportsmanship.

After Kiski's second contest Mathias and Harry Stuhldreher, Jr. were brought to Pittsburgh to address the Quarterback Club at its weekly luncheon and to be introduced to Golden Triangle sports experts. When called on to say a few words about his great decathlon conquest, Bob stood up and said: "It was a privilege to take part in the Olympics." Then he sat down again. Observing this, Lester J. Biederman of the *Pittsburgh Press* wrote: "Jack Armstrong, the mythical All-American Boy, has a deadly serious rival."

In its homecoming game against the powerful Cornell freshmen, Kiski suffered its first defeat, 24-0, despite the valiant efforts of the home team. Aided by Bob's running, Kiski rolled up eleven first downs to the visitors' four, but it couldn't dent the heavier Big Red line for a score.

The next week Kiski rebounded to turn back the strong Western Reserve frosh, 17-13. Bob accounted for his side's final touchdown by intercepting a pass and galloping twenty yards.

As the season wore on Coach Marks admitted that Mathias had more than fulfilled expectations, and Bob was enjoying the game so much he began to change his mind about concentrating on track at the expense of football at Stanford.

"He's a great help to a coach," Marks told a press gathering. "His spirit is excellent and I can't say enough for him.

"He's not a spectacular runner yet, but his value as a blocker and a line backer-up has earned my thanks in all our games. Bob is hampered by a slow start and his long stride makes it tough for him to get through the opposing line, but the punishment he gives opposing tacklers has paid off. After he finishes a couple of periods of softening the opposition, I put in my second string fullback, a conventional plunger, and usually we can coast. Mathias does his best work on the outside.

119

He moves that big frame of his with great speed and he's a tough customer in the open."

News of Bob's continuous improvement tickled Stanford alumni, as well as Tulareans. The former could hardly wait for him to enroll, as Stanford's football fortunes were at an ebb.

In Kiski's remaining three games Bob was also to add to his reputation as a ball hawk. Against Grove City College freshmen Bob intercepted a pass and ran it back fifteen yards to score as his team triumphed, 20-0.

In the second quarter of the tilt with the West Virginia freshmen, Bob hauled in an enemy aerial and hotfooted it back sixty-two yards to the end zone to enable his club to win, 7-6.

In the closeout against Mercersberg Academy, Kiski outgained and outplayed its traditional rival, but was beaten, 26-6, by costly fumbles. The Mathias-led Kiski attack had ten first downs to five for Mercersberg, but at critical intervals it stalled.

With football season over, Bob was in for further honors. Tulare was awarded the 1949 national decathlon meet largely on the basis of Bob's statement that he would defend his title if the affair were held in his home town.

Then Bob was invited to attend the first annual Banquet of Champions at Toledo. The affair, held December 17, 1948, was sponsored by R. A. Stranahan, noted automotive supply executive and sportsman, to honor twenty-four of the nation's top athletes. The dinner was unique in that it was designed strictly for the enjoyment of the athletes, who were freed of all speech-

Bob on his first birth-
day, November 17,
1931.

A man of the Old West (aged four).

e Mathias boys: Eu-
e, 9; Robert, 6;
my, 3.

Bob says goodbye to a
pal as he leaves for his
first day of school.

In training for the Rose
Bowl Game of 1952.

The Freshman Basketball Team, Tulare High. Bob is third from the left in the back row.

At sixteen and a half Bob threw the discus 150′ 8¾″ to set a new high school record. Here his friends congratulate him.

In the broad jump at the 1948 Olympics (London) Bob reached 21' 8⅓".

United Press Photo

A mighty 144′ 4″ discus throw tops the field in
this event in the 1948 Olympic decathlon.

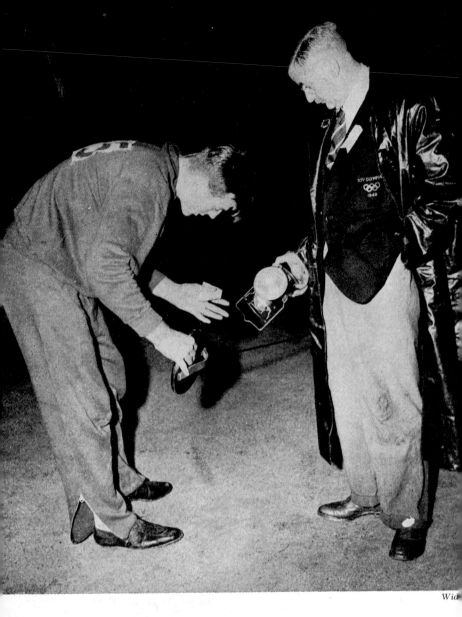

Darkness required Bob to measure his runs
by flashlight for the javelin throw at
London.

The first heat in the 110 meter hurdles, London, 1948.

Wide World

A new world's champion thanks his mother.

European

The victory ceremony at Wembley Stadium,
August 7, 1948.

The champion saved a special greeting for a special friend.

Tulare turns out to welcome a victor.

Curley Grieve

Joe Daniel Payne hawks Tulare's big news of 1948.

Just one of Tulare's tributes to Bob.

Bob returns Western Reserve's kickoff for Kiski.

Setting a new prep school high hurdle record, Spring, 1949.

President Truman congratulates Bob Mathias and Arthur Cook, winners of the Olympic decathlon and small rifle titles.

James A. Rhodes awards Bob Mathias the James E. Sullivan Award, the nation's highest tribute to an amateur athlete.

 orld

Stanford's fullback breaks away for a gain
against California, November 24, 1951.

United Press-Acme Photo

Mathias stiff arms an opponent as he powers through for another long Stanford gain.

A basketball star also, Bob is
never too busy to give tips to
young hopefuls.

Wherever Bob goes, crowds
of young admirers surround
him.

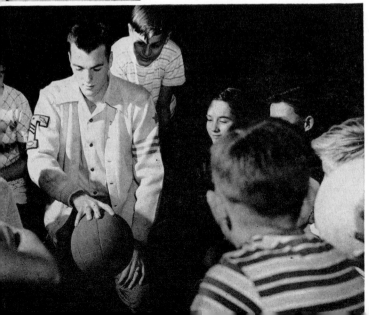

Bob and his sister Patricia relax in the Trophy
Room of the Mathias home.

Tulare's first family. *Left to right:* Patricia, Jim,
Bob, Gene and his wife Priscilla, with Dr. and
Mrs. Mathias.

High jump (6′ ¾″)

1500 meter (5.05 min.)

Javelin (182′ 4½″)

140

Edwin Schober

Pole vault (13′ ¾″)

Schober

Ray Snider

Discus (146′ 5″)

Shot put (47′ 6¼″)

In Bern, Switzerland, (1950) Bob rewards his young admirers with bubble gum sent by his mother.

Bob Mathias prepares to defend his Olympic Decathlon Championship title in Helsinki, Finland, 1952.

Keystone

Bob gets away fast at the start of the 100 meter dash at Helsinki.

rough the air for a leap of 22' 10.8" in the broad jump.

ystone

The shot put at Helsinki. Bob has written in his lucky number 11 on his official Olympic numeral.

With his injured thigh heavily bandaged Bob records the good time of 14.7 seconds in the 110 meter hurdles.

The pole vault is Bob's most difficult event because of his weight. Here he clears the bar at Helsinki at 13' 1.16".

Olympia Kuva Oy

In the next to last event of the 1952 Olympic decathlon Bob
hurled the javelin 194' 3.15" to assure himself of a new world's
record.

149

The ordeal is over. Bob is one
step from victory as night set-
tles on the 1952 Olympics.

Bob Mathias helps Milton Campbell, runner up in the 1952 Olym
after a gruelling race.

The world's best. *Left to right:* Floyd Simmons, third in the 1952 Olympics with 6,788 points; Bob Mathias,

making or autograph-signing for others. The signatures they signed this time were for their fellow athletes.

Bob, the apple-cheeked prepster, shared champion billing with twenty-three older, longer-established heroes, including Joe Di Maggio, Ben Hogan, Charlie Justice, Jack Kramer, Bob Kurland, George Mikan, Stan Musial, Ted Schroeder, Frank Stranahan, son of the sponsor, and Charlie Trippi. Along with the others, Bob was spotlighted before the 250 guests, called to the stage, presented with a new movie camera, and ushered to a seat on the platform.

Bob returned to Tulare for Christmas vacation and a well deserved visit with his family. While in Tulare he was asked to be a guest at a Christmas theater party sponsored by the Elks Club for the children of Tulare. As Santa came on stage, the kids roared and screamed their approval. When Bob was introduced, however, the youngsters paid him the ultimate in homage; they doubled the applause they had given Santa. Dick Wegener, the emcee, reminded the kids, "Only a couple of years ago, Bob was sitting down there where you are and now he is the Olympic decathlon champion and the greatest all-around athlete of all time."

As a token of esteem, officials representing the California Interscholastic Federation, governing body of the state's high school athletics, presented Bob with a gold life-time pass to all CIF games in ceremonies broadcast over Tulare station KCOK. It was the first of its kind ever to be given by the notoriously conservative CIF, and possibly the last. The pass was decided upon in preference to some other type of award because Bob's house was already overflowing with trophies.

Maxwell Stiles, sports editor of the *Los Angeles Mirror,* visited the Mathiases for Christmas and he wrote of it as the "Typical American Yuletide":

". . . There was all the true joy of a typical American yuletide in this splendid American home, for they were all together glowing in their pride that one of their number, eighteen-year-old Robert, had become famed as the greatest all-around athlete in the world.

"Robert was home for the holidays, home from Kiski, where he is prepping for entrance in Stanford University next fall. Big brother Gene . . . was home from Palo Alto, where he is a senior in pre-med. Jimmy, almost fifteen, and sister Patricia . . . complete one of the finest family groups that are spending Christmas together anywhere in this broad land of ours.

"Robert, the boy wonder of the Olympics . . . divided his time today among the pleasures of sleeping, drinking quarts and quarts of milk, opening Christmas presents and being the genuine pal of the neighborhood small fry. Every kid in Tulare county between the ages of five and seventeen is out to become another Bob Mathias. They all do what he did, train as he trained, eat what he ate, don't smoke because he doesn't smoke. The kids of grammar and junior high school age are his devoted slaves. Bob is their idol and their god.

"I have never come upon a case in which one young man has exerted so great an influence over the five-to-fifteen-year-olds of a community as Bob Mathias does in the town of Tulare. Some of the more sophisticated high school lads and town punks are not so highly impressed. But the small fry, the pollywogs, are finding in Bob Mathias an inspiration and a goal, a beacon light toward which they have set a course that is certain to steer them away from the paths of delinquency and ever onward toward becoming the finest athletes and the finest young men that it is within their power to become.

"Bob Mathias was one of a handful of athletes nominated for the Sullivan Award, based on athletic achievement plus sportsmanship. I do not know whether he will win, but I do know that no man who ever won the Sullivan Award in the past ever deserved it more. No American athlete has ever done more to promote sportsmanship and good citizenship than Bob Mathias has done, and is doing, in the entire San Joaquin valley.

"Mrs. Mathias . . . deserves a special award as the mother of the year in American sports. This lovely woman with the ash-blond hair, the nimble wit, and the tireless energy, has brought into this world four of the most wonderful youngsters you will find anywhere. And she has brought them up right, in a good, clean, Christian home, a home that has been a sort of a gymnasium and a playground for all the neighborhood kids ever since Gene was a little boy.

"Mrs. Mathias is president of the Cherry Avenue Junior High School PTA. She lectures on sportsmanship and the Olympics. She goes to all the games, just as the very wise and kindly father, Dr. Mathias, goes to all the games as the team doctor and sits with the Tulare High school squad on the bench.

155

"Big, good-natured Gene was . . . strong enough to throw the regular college discus 139 feet. Eager, ambitious Jimmy puts the 8-pound shot farther than any kid in the county and is set on making a future Olympic team . . .

"There have been no late hours in the Mathias family. The kids have always been home in bed by 8:30 or 9 o'clock. The doctor and his wife knew and still know where they are. The result of that is reflected in the clean-cut faces, the clear eyes, the healthy physiques and the athletic achievements of their offspring.

"Coach Virgil Jackson . . . who was the first to get the idea that Robert could make the decathlon team, and who trained him to become a world all-around champion, drops by to exchange Christmas gifts. Jackson . . . gets my vote as high school coach of the year. Maybe he is the high school track coach of all time. Bob Mathias and Simeon Iness, the discus thrower, are good recommendations for such an honor.

"As Jackson comes up the walk toward the Mathias home . . . he finds the windows blacked out with Christmas-colored paper. A huge cardboard Santa Claus and Xmas cards bearing the words, *'From Us to You,'* give him . . . a merry greeting. Kids from all around the town are brought over to the Mathias home just to see Santa Claus . . .

". . . It is because I think the Mathiases of Tulare form the No. 1 family group of the year in California that I have singled out their little home for a very special 'Merry Christmas' . . . Our nation and our state need more families like this . . .

156

"Thank you, Mrs. Mathias, gracious lady, for this gift of a true Christmas to the people of California and America."

The family discussed the Sullivan Award over their turkey, but Bob said: "I don't think it's for me this time. Gene and I think Harrison Dillard ought to win it. He sure made a great comeback at London. He was runner-up for the award last year and he surely deserves it this time."

The winner had not yet been announced when Bob left to attend the *Los Angeles Times* Sports Award dinner at which he was named "outstanding track athlete of 1948." He was one of twenty-one champions in their own field honored before more than a thousand sports, screen, and stage celebrities.

Just after the close of 1948, "The Year of Mathias," as Noyes Alexander of the *Tulare Advance-Register* termed it, when Bob already had departed for Kiski, he was voted amateur sportsdom's most cherished accolade, the James E. Sullivan Memorial Award.

The honor, set up in 1939 in the name of the man who organized the present national Amateur Athletic Union, is given annually to the amateur "who, by performance, example and good influence, did most to advance the cause of good sportsmanship during the year."

Mathias got 201 first place votes out of 252 ballots cast by sports leaders throughout the United States. Dillard, who was second with 119 first place votes, had won the Olympic 100 meters title after failing in his specialty, the hurdles, in the national tryouts. Bob won over four other candidates, the only six left on the ballot after the nominees of 43 district associations had been screened by the award committee at the AAU's annual meeting in New York.

Hy Turkin, a New York sports writer, had prophesied Bob would win when he wrote, a few days before the selection: "Though the Sullivan Award is supposed to be based just as much on sportsmanship as physical prowess, the muscular often overshadows the spiritual ... but Mathias rates high no matter what the standard."

The news of his selection as winner of the Sullivan Award came to Bob Mathias at 3:30 P.M. on January 5, 1949. At the close of the day's classes President Clark's secretary was waiting outside the classroom door to summon him to the headmaster's office. The news that was waiting for him there was, he said, "the nicest thing that ever happened to me."

Flashbulbs started popping and cameras clicked. Bob merely helped himself to some nuts on the President's desk, and stuffed the used flashbulbs into his pockets for souvenirs.

Mathias' citation read:

> Winner of the Olympic, National AAU and Pacific Coast decathlon championships is the unique record established by this 17½ year old youth [Bob still was not 18 when nominated]. He was an outstanding performer in track, basketball and football while attending Tulare High School and was twice selected as the meritorious performer at the Fresno West Coast Relays. He competed in the gruelling decathlon event for the first time in

the Pacific Coast championships last June and won with a point total of 7,094, the highest total score in this event in the United States since 1941. Three weeks later he won the National AAU Championships with 7,224 points on a rain soaked field. Five weeks later at the Olympic Games he triumphed over the world's greatest all-around athletes.

His extreme modesty, his excellent sportsmanship and his terrific competitive spirit have endeared him to all followers of sport. He is strictly a team player. When urged by the coach of the U.S. Olympic track and field team to refrain from basketball and high school track competition to concentrate on the decathlon, he refused since he felt that he could not let his teammates down.

Is now attending Kiski Prep School, Saltsburg, Pa. Intends to drop football and concentrate on pole vault, shot put and discus and is looking forward to defending his Olympic title at Helsinki in 1952.

Bob, now leading Kiski's track team to the greatest season it ever enjoyed, was presented with the award in New York in February, 1949. Mrs. Mathias, who was with him, declared, "I'm thrilled that this high honor should come to one so young."

Bob declared simply, "This is my second greatest thrill. My first came at London last summer. I only hope that I can live up to what this award stands for."

That spring at the National Scholastic meet in New York, which decides the prep school track championship, Bob won the 60-yard hurdles, and placed second in the high jump and broad jump. He accounted for all but two of Kiski's eighteen points as it finished second in team scoring.

Mathias would have done better but for another mixup. Appearing at Madison Square Garden for the afternoon meet, he was refused admittance for lack of a ticket.

"You were supposed to get a ticket with your mailed instructions," the doorman said.

Bob said he never had received either. Finally Dan Ferris, AAU secretary, had to be called to identify him and pass him in. Then Bob learned that the instructions which he had never received listed the shot put, in which he also was entered, for that morning at a New York high school.

Bob had industriously applied himself to his books. He finished his year at Kiski among the first twenty in his class and qualified for Stanford.

After a brief vacation Bob began to prepare to defend his national decathlon title. At Tulare High Stadium later that summer he was challenged by competitors, but, on his home grounds, and with the townsfolk giving him lusty vocal support, the weather warm and at the peak of condition, he proved invincible. He rolled up 7,556 points, more than he ever had done before.

That summer he went on a tour of the Scandinavian countries with a group of American athletes. At Oslo, Norway, he forgot his track shoes in his hotel room and had to borrow from a fellow athlete a pair that cramped his feet. But even with his toes curled up, Bob copped the "Little Olympics" decathlon with 7,346 points, defeating a tough entry that included Moon Mondschein and Billy Albans of the U.S., Oern Claussen of Iceland and Paul Ericsson of Sweden.

On that junket Bob playfully got even with Mondschein for having kept him awake most of the way over to London the previous year. It is one of Bob's favorite stories:

"Moon and Bill Albans and I shared the same room and somehow they got the idea I had some secret formula for relaxing. So they watched me like hawks. Every time I flopped down for a snooze, they did, too. My bedtime was their bedtime. When I hit the deck in the morning, so did they. When I finally got hep to what they were thinking, I started driving them crazy with ridiculous maneuvers. I kept a split-second schedule. I'd doze for ten minutes, get up, drink a glass of water, doze for ten more minutes, and start all meals exactly on the hour or half-hour. They followed me like they were under Army orders. I'll bet to this day they still think, 'That guy Mathias sure has a crazy way of training.'"

That trip was the last on which Mathias could be billed as "the prep school kid." The college phase of his career was about to begin.

Chapter 8

DOWN ON "THE FARM"

Long before he moved to the lovely grounds of Stanford University, with its low, Spanish-style buildings clustered under the sighing eucalyptus trees against a backdrop of hazy, purple hills, Bob Mathias was a BMOC—Big Man on Campus.

He was the most sought-after catch of every fraternity rushing committee. And the determination with which the coeds set their pincurls and tacked up his picture on their walls indicated that he rated as the prize catch among the sororities, too. Athletic Director Al Masters and the coaches of every major sport began sharing a recurrently pleasant dream—the seasons would change, but the name of the versatile Mathias would remain in the lineup. Seldom had "The Farm," as Stanford is affectionately known, or, for that matter, any other college seen a more reluctant BMOC.

Hardly had Mathias registered than everyone found out that here was one celebrity who was really different. Instead of feverishly branching out into a variety of activities, like the typical campus big shot, Bob retired into a shell. He was seen more often in the Stanford Chapel than at public gatherings, and he caused some deep disappointment among Stanford alumni and sports followers when, in that autumn of 1949, he did not even turn out for freshman football.

This decision was influenced by Gene Mathias, then a Stanford senior. Some speculated that Gene had warned Bob against football because of the near-tragic gridiron accident he himself had suffered in high school. Others saw it as a fear on Bob's part that a football injury would halt his track career, which he relished more. Bob denied this, saying: "The worst that ever happened to me is getting knocked breathless, so why should I be worried?"

The real reason, however, had nothing to do with sports. Both boys had once hoped to set up as partners with their father in his medical practice in and around Tulare. When Gene, a better scholar than Bob, failed to make a good enough record to gain admittance to medical school and had to switch to medical administration, he insisted that Bob, at least in his first college semester, should concentrate on his books before anything else.

"First get your grades," Gene counseled his brother. "Then you can go out for sports." Bob, who followed Gene in almost everything, took his advice.

In choosing fraternities, though, the brothers went different ways. Gene was a member of Sigma Nu, but because he would be leaving soon and Bob had some close friends who liked Phi Gamma Delta—among them Bob Hoegh, his old Tulare High and Kiski team-mate;

Dick Borda of San Jose; and Jim Agar, of Santa Monica, brother of film star John Agar—he pledged Phi Gamma Delta.

Shortly after he joined Phi Gamma Delta, the Fijis, as members of this fraternity are known, decided to test the character of their famous acquisition. They handed him a brush and a bucket and told him: "Here, Bob, the floors need washing." Every eye in the place intently watched his reaction. Without a word of comment, the young man who had shaken hands with the President, had stood on an Olympic victory stand, and had been lauded around the earth, accepted the implements and got down on his hands and knees with the other freshmen and scrubbed the floor.

From then on, Bob was in—and his reputation for being a regular guy grew with the passing days. His fraternity brothers praised him for his thoughtfulness. John McDonald, son of the San Francisco sports editor, Jack McDonald, and a roommate of Mathias, revealed to his father: "Bob always sets the alarm clock for me every night before we go to bed. I borrow his tooth paste and he borrows my shaving cream. He's always thinking of the other fellow." The Fijis got to like him so well, in fact, that they eventually elected him to the all-important position of chairman of their rushing committee, so that he would have a decisive voice in screening potential members.

Fan mail continued to pour in on him and he used his own money to fill requests for pictures. It never occurred to him that Don Liebendorfer, head of the University's athletic publicity department, would have been only too glad to meet such expenses. To his mother he complained: "Heck, Mom, I'd answer all of these letters, but half the time they leave off a return address."

Bob cracked the books hard that first college term, but still the courses were pretty stiff and his grades showed a "C" average. The next spring he made Stanford sports partisans breathe a bit easier when he reported for freshman track.

What he did will probably never be done again by a yearling wearing the cardinal and white. He shattered four all-time freshman standards—in the discus, the shot, the high hurdles and the pole vault. In the Little Big Meet with California's frosh he took five firsts and tallied more than a third of his side's total, 28 of 74 points. In five dual meets he averaged three first places, and over the entire season he totaled 89 1/3 points—practically a team in himself.

Still improving in all events, Mathias hoped, in June of 1950, to reward his home town with his best-yet performance in the decathlon when he defended his title for the second time. But the first night Billy Albans got off to a flying start; he sprinted the 100 meters in 10.6 seconds, broad jumped more than 24 feet, high jumped more than six feet and raced the 400 meters in 49.4 seconds. At the end of the first five events Albans had a big lead over Mathias, and Tulareans were frowning.

"I'm scared," a friend told Bob. "How are you going to catch up?"

"Oh, I've just been figuring points," Bob said. "My

second night will be better. I know if I can do my best,
I'll be okay."

The next day he was slightly more than okay. He
sped over the 110 meter high hurdles faster than he
ever had done before—14.7 seconds. He whipped the
discus 146 feet, cleared 13 feet in the pole vault—a new
high in decathlon annals—tailed off somewhat in the
javelin and 1500 meters, but still swamped the flabber-
gasted Albans by 681 points. His terrific surge gave him
a sensational 8,042 points and finally broke Glenn Morris' world record of 7,900 that had stood unchallenged
for fourteen years.

Commenting on the way Mathias spurted past him,
the stunned Albans said: "When I saw that movie about
The Thing which defied destruction, I thought of
Mathias. You can't beat him. He isn't human."

Albans, however, was only using a figure of speech.
If there was anything Mathias continued to be noted for
after that it was his human qualities. As a sophomore,
he again caused disillusionment among Stanford partisans by not reporting for football, but at his fraternity
he uncomplainingly did all of the menial tasks which
are the lot of an underclassman.

He dated occasionally, but, as in sports, he played
the field. (On dates he prefers to go to the movies or to
go dancing at a quiet place. He dances well and likes
an ordinary tune rather than a rumba, samba, or swing
number.) Besides, his habit of early hours, in season and
out, prevented him from being much of a social lion.
He remained loyal to his original ambition to pursue a
medical career and that fall, instead of butting his head

against tackling dummies, he cracked his brains against such tough subjects as sociology, chemistry, biology, and psychology. He avidly read all the medical literature he could lay his hands on, not only to keep abreast of developments in the field, but because he had early learned the value of an intimate knowledge of the wonderful machine that was his body in maintaining his health and improving his track and field marks.

Bob kept in shape by constantly exercising and competing in intramural sports, but somewhere between the fall of 1950 and the spring of 1951, when he started his first varsity season of track, he picked up a mysterious muscle spasm in his back.

Because of his injury and in order to be of maximum help to his team, Bob concentrated on only three events: the discus, shot put and low hurdles. In the 1951 Pacific Coast Conference-Big Ten dual meet at Eugene, Oregon, he set an all-time Stanford high in the discus with a winning throw of 173 feet, 4 inches. In the NCAA meet at Seattle his second in the discus and sixth in the shot accounted for all nine of the Stanford Indians' points. Throughout the dual meet season he was a consistent point-earner in the three events he entered.

Mathias' average of 51 feet, 2 inches in the shot put caused one newly-converted track enthusiast to comment to Coach Jack Weiershauser: "Gee, he sure has good form, hasn't he?"

"No, he's still got plenty to learn," Weiershauser answered. "He doesn't get down low enough and he hasn't the speed across the ring that you'd expect him to have."

"Then how does he do it?" asked the flustered fan.

"Well," said Weiershauser, scratching his head, "he just does it, that's all. Especially when we need it. It's all in his mind."

During that spring Bob, now a draft eligible, joined the Marines' Platoon Leaders Course at Stanford, which would permit him to stay in school and give him a chance at a Marines commission. This required Bob to put in two summers at boot camp before qualifying for officer's training. The desire to get one of them out of the way immediately and the fact that he had limited himself to three events during the season, influenced Mathias to forego defending his national decathlon title. That summer at San Diego he got his first taste of something just as rugged—Marine basic training.

As Bob entered his junior year of college, he still had not raised his marks much above a "C" average, despite all his hard work. Reluctantly, but realistically, he abandoned his hope of becoming a doctor. "I just couldn't make the grades," Bob frankly admitted. And in the fall of 1951 he decided to try his hand at college football.

There were visible bulges in the cheeks of the sideliners when Mathias asked for a suit. He had not played football for two years, the last time being at Kiski, and he had not even had the benefit of spring practice. "We know this guy's good—in track," was the consensus of opinion. "But just who does he think he is trying to move in on the football varsity without any college experience?"

Stanford was not highly regarded in pre-season forecasts, but the squad was liberally sprinkled with lettermen and there were two good ones ahead of Mathias at fullback. That was an old story, however, with the Tulare whiz. Tight-lipped, he went to work. At first the experts seemed to be right. It took Bob time to recover the feel of the game. He hesitated in hitting the line as though he were looking around for the hole; and when a hole did open quickly, he was slow going through it. Worse, he didn't last out the first scrimmage. He fractured his toe and was forced out of action for five days.

The experts were having a field day. Mathias was a track man trying to become a gridder. You needed different muscles for football than you did for track, they said. His long stride kept him from cutting sharply, they observed, and his center of gravity was so high that he would be brought down easily.

When Bob came back to practice, he immediately reinjured the toe. Back he went on the inactive list for another week. The chorus of criticism grew louder: "He can't take it." "He's too brittle for football." "He doesn't know how to protect himself." "He'll quit to save himself for track."

After a week, when Mathias got back into the thick of things, he pulled up with a sore thigh muscle. Having had very little opportunity to impress the coach, he was left off the traveling squad for the opening game with Oregon at Portland. As far as the grandstand quarterbacks were concerned, that proved they had been right all along about Mathias. It was a hard blow to a lad who had known global fame, but Bob didn't let it get him down.

The next Monday, after Stanford had unimpressively squeaked by weak Oregon, 27-20, Mathias was out on the practice lot, laboring as hard as ever. He still wasn't far enough along at the end of the week to be used against San Jose State, even though the Indians did not have too much trouble winning, 26-13. As so many rival athletes had found out to their dismay, so did the scoffers finally discover that Bob was not one to give up easily.

At last Mathias made the traveling roster for the game against Michigan at Ann Arbor. The Wolverines were slightly favored, but Chuck Taylor, the likable, optimistic redhead making his debut as Stanford head coach, predicted a Cardinal victory. "These kids want to win," Taylor said.

It was the birth of a famous rallying cry. Because of his speed, Mathias was used as deep man on kickoff returns. He ran one back seventeen yards and another eleven and did not see further duty. But Stanford surprised the Big Ten team, 23-13, and its spirit really began to lift.

Recapping the game, Taylor said: "Mathias has a long way to go before he'll be of help. Maybe I'll shift him to right half for insurance there."

During the first scrimmage of the week in preparation for UCLA, Bob Meyers and Skip Crist, the two men ahead of Mathias at fullback, were injured; and Bob, with only five days of real practice and two varsity plays behind him, stepped into the first string fullback job.

Despite the crippling injuries, Taylor remained optimistic. "It's our toughest one yet," he said, "but we'll do all right. We'll miss Meyers, but I'll put my money on Mathias." As he had done so often before, Mathias arrived in time, scoring two touchdowns as Stanford defeated UCLA, one of the favorites in the race, 21-7.

After UCLA tied the count at 7-7 in the third quarter, Bob bucked over what proved to be the winning score and then in the fourth period sparked a long drive by breaking away for 27 yards and finally crashing over from the one.

Despite the fact that Mathias' football feats were making him an even more popular campus figure than he was before, Coach Taylor and other observers remained cautious. "The rating of Mathias shouldn't be hurried," Taylor said. "He's on his way, but the way is long and tough. He'll have to do a lot more at fullback to take the job away from Meyers and Crist, who are experienced players."

As long as Bob could feel that he was making his maximum contribution to the team effort of the amazing Indians, he was not too concerned about his role. There had been those who maintained that Mathias' success in sports had been due to his detached attitude, the fact that he could view a contest as merely a good workout that provided a lot of clean fun, but was nothing more than that. Many interpreted his coolness under fire as indifference.

These allegations were not without a germ of truth. In action, Mathias did not, like many athletes, show the contorted face, the reckless physical abandon of a gladiator staking his life on every movement within the arena. From track Bob had come to value pace, and pace meant sometimes going at half-speed if that would insure the proper sprint at the finish. Behind his spirit Bob tried to put as much science as possible. As his high school coach Virgil Jackson commented, "Bob gets keyed up but he makes it work for him, not against him."

When Stanford's victory string began to lengthen, Bob's composure was visibly affected. "Yes, they're really getting me," Bob confided to a fraternity brother. "In track I'm on my own. I help no one and no one helps me. In football it's something else again. We're a team. Everyone of us is dependent on the others. You can feel the spirit. When we started our upsets we all got a terrific lift. I think we're playing over our heads because we all don't want to let the others down."

Just before the next game, with Santa Clara, Mathias suffered a slight charley horse, but it didn't prevent him from bearing the brunt of the Stanford attack.

As usual the Broncos were high for the battle with their bigger neighbors. Stanford scored first on a 79-yard drive capped by Mathias' 4-yard slice over guard, but Santa Clara got that touchdown back in the second quarter, and the half ended in a 7-7 deadlock.

Again, in the third period, the rivals swapped touchdowns. Then, late in the final quarter, with an embarrassing tie staring them in the face, the Indians got a march going from their own 37-yard line. With the ball on the Broncos' 18 and only two minutes remaining, Mathias' signal was called, and the Tulare touchdown express roared inside end for the full distance to the goal line. The final tally was 21-14.

Then Stanford traveled to Seattle to bait the tough Washington Huskies in their own lair. This, it was generally conceded, was the beginning of the critical phase of Stanford's schedule. It was a close, bruising battle, but thanks to Mathias' efforts, Stanford won, 14-7. Bob even outshone the Huskies' vaunted All-American fullback candidate, Hugh McElhenny. The latter outgained Mathias, but Mathias delivered better in the clutch and for the first time impressed everyone as a blocker too.

From the kickoff Stanford rolled 72 yards to a touchdown and within minutes, after recovering a Washington fumble, had another scoring chance. Gary Kerkorian passed 14 yards to Mathias who caught the ball on the one and went over, but the play was nullified by a holding penalty, and Stanford was stopped. Late in the first half the Cards had another touchdown called back because they were offside.

In the third quarter McElhenny broke away for 69 yards to tie the score, but in the final period, from its own 33, Stanford uncorked the deciding drive. Mathias sparked the advance by breaking 33 yards through tackle on a pitchout. The Cards were temporarily set back by a holding penalty, but fought their way to the Washington five yard line. With fourth down and two yards to go they relied on Mathias. He didn't fail. He crashed through for three yards and a first down on the two yard line. The next play carried over the goal line, and the Indians remained unbeaten.

After that one, Bob grinned: "I'm beginning to like football almost as much as I do track, even though it's costing me all the skin off my nose." His running was being credited for preventing the opposition from ganging up on the Gary Kerkorian-to-Bill McColl passing combination, Stanford's most explosive weapon.

In the following week's encounter with Washington State at Palo Alto, Mathias' ball-packing again was a feature as the Cards rolled up an early 21-0 lead and coasted to victory, 21-13. Bob punched out an average of 4.5 yards on 13 carries as Stanford unreeled scoring drives of 46, 57 and 80 yards. Not in years had Stanford supporters watched an Indian eleven that could put together drives like this team. Seventeen times during the season they had marched fifty yards or more to the end zone.

The next date on the Stanford football calendar, with beefy Southern California at Los Angeles, was its toughest assignment yet. The Trojans, after having dealt California its first regular season defeat since 1947, were favorites in the conference race. True, the Cards were still undefeated, but they had not yet collided with the likes of man-eating USC. A win for either side would practically assure the victor of representing the PCC in the Rose Bowl and the importance of the struggle almost filled the 100,000 seats of the Los Angeles Memorial Coliseum to capacity.

Stanford capitalized on an early break when it recovered a fumble close to the USC goal line and scored on a pass for a 7-0 lead. The clubs rocked and socked for the rest of the first half, but without changing the scoreboard.

After the intermission the Trojans came out steaming mad and immediately crunched 73 yards in eight plays. Frank Gifford, USC's All-American quarterback, went the last 18 yards and kicked the conversion to tie the game. Later in the quarter Johnny Williams, the fleet Trojan safety man, took a punt on his own 22 and appeared headed for another touchdown. At the last minute a huge figure came galloping up behind him and, with a last-ditch tackle, crashed him to earth on the Stanford 24. It was none other than Tulare's favorite son. Inspired by Mathias' deed, the Indians dug in and held and USC missed a field goal attempt.

The pressure was mounting. After an exchange of punts, USC swished 65 yards and a touchdown in five tries to take the lead, 14-7, early in the fourth quarter. It appeared as if the Trojans had finally asserted their superiority and were permanently in command of the ball game.

They kicked off to Stanford. Mathias caught it on the four yard line and, behind teammate Wes Laubscher, started straight up field. Crisp blocks rubbed out the first Trojans down under the kick and Mathias kept picking up speed. Around the 35 yard line, Laubscher threw a key block and Mathias saw daylight. He cut toward the sideline at his right, but he was still not out of trouble. At midfield two speedy Trojans, Gifford and Williams, were bearing down on him. Mathias opened the throttle. He zipped by Williams, but Gifford dove. He missed, falling flat on his face. Bob, close to the sideline, almost lost his balance and stepped out of bounds, but he recovered and continued on to the goal line unmolested. The giant stadium shook with excitement. Bob's gleeful mates hugged him.

A groan went up from the Stanford side when Gary Kerkorian missed the subsequent conversion, but it was still 14-13 and Stanford had its needed lift and was back in the ball game.

The pitch of the battle mounted. Now USC struck back, fighting its way down to the Stanford one yard line. The aroused Indians braced and held, but then Kerkorian, trying to pass from his goal line, was tackled and dropped the ball, and Troy recovered in the end zone to go ahead 20-13. It would have been 21-13, but the conversion was erased by a penalty and the next kick went awry.

The Cards were not giving up, however. A few plays after the following kickoff they launched another drive, partially aided by penalties. A long pass carried them to the enemy 13, and when USC was penalized five yards for delaying the game the ball was placed on the 8. Stanford rooters were madly yelling: "We want a touchdown! We want a touchdown!"

There was not much time remaining. In such a critical situation, who else would the Stanford signal callers think of but Mathias? Bob hit the line and wound up on the five yard line. The Troy defense tightened up, expecting another line smash. They were right, but they

177

still couldn't stop the Tulare bulldozer. He barged through to the one.

Now the Troy defenders, their backs to the wall and anticipating another line buck, really closed in, poised to smash the play.

Again they had guessed right, but again they were no match for a determined Mathias. He knifed into the line and scored standing up. This time Kerkorian's place kick was true and with the count deadlocked at 20-20 the Stanford stands were in an uproar.

Only minutes remained and USC, seeking a clean-cut decision, began passing. Skip Crist, Stanford back, intercepted one and returned it 31 yards to the USC 11. Mathias drove to the 9. A pass ate up three more yards and then Harry Hugasian plunged the final six to the end zone. The play was called back, and Stanford penalized for offsides. With the ball on the 11, Hugasian ripped off ten yards and then, with an undeniable momentum, banged through center for the touchdown.

The conversion was good, making the final tally, 27-20. With a Rose Bowl invitation practically cinched, the Stanford cheering section went berserk. If there had still been doubts about Mathias' greatness as a football player, this game dispelled them.

Afterwards, the Stanford dressing room was a bedlam of shouting, singing, steam, tape, and ointment. When Bob emerged from the shower, he was mobbed by reporters and admirers. They asked him about that 96-yard gallop.

"It was nothing," Bob said quietly, as he dried himself. And, characteristically, he gave most of the credit to his helpers. "Great blocking did it. Two of the fellows took out the end and another knocked down a tackle and that left a big hole anyone could have run through."

"But, Bob," someone objected, "what about those two guys you left flatfooted when they were closing in on you at midfield?"

However, Mathias was already answering another question: "What were you thinking about on that run?" Bob smiled. "Only about going toward the goal line."

A reporter winced. "Gad, there's no getting any color out of him."

Bob did provide a little color, however. The grinning and talking and wiping his face had opened the old scratch on his nose and blood trickled down. He wiped it with the towel. Then he tried to get out of the crowd by saying, "I guess I ought to go get the tape off my ankles."

As he began to strip off the tape he noticed that he had forgotten to shave his legs before the game. "Boy," he winced, "this is worse than getting bumped in the game."

The crowd closed in on him again. "Why did you come out for football this season, Bob?" someone asked.

"Well, I love to play and couldn't see any reason for not playing this fall." To reassure the track bugs, he added, "As soon as football is over I'll start working toward the Olympics again." Then, thinking of the grid fans, he said, "After that, though, I hope to play more football."

"What did you get a bigger thrill out of, winning the

decathlon or scoring that touchdown?" a reporter queried.

"Gee, you can't compare them," Bob answered. "They're different. Every touchdown's a kick, and so is winning three or four events in track or beating some good competitor."

By now the tumult had died down, Bob was dressed and wanted to go. When the group around Mathias broke up and joined the knot around Coach Taylor, they heard him say, "Actually Bob hadn't looked too good in practice before the game."

"Yeah, but how was that run for distance, coach?" cracked Paul Zimmerman, sports editor of the *Los Angeles Times*.

Prescott Sullivan, the *San Francisco Examiner* sports writer, viewed Bob's antics as inevitable. He wrote: "The Trojans might just as well have kicked off to Frank Merriwell or Tom Rover as kick off to Mathias in the action-packed fourth quarter when they were only a touchdown ahead. It was a mistake which must have sent recollections of their boyhood reading swimming before the Trojans' eyes.

"Mathias took the ball on his own four-yard line and ran it back 96 yards to a TD even as Merriwell or Rover surely would have done. It just couldn't have happened any other way. Not in a game like this one with the old school pleading for heroics. Bob Mathias, the Olympic decathlon champion, was born to save the day."

Tulareans, though, weren't too surprised. "He'd done it so often in high school," one said, "we'd come to expect it."

Stanford still had to get by its next foe, Oregon State, to sew up the conference championship. It was Mathias' twenty-first birthday and he celebrated by tallying two more touchdowns and doing most of the work in a third payoff drive as the Cards triumphed, 35-14. However, the victory was costly. Bob picked up a hip injury that prevented him from doing much practicing for the annual Big Game with California.

Before that traditional contest, Bob again demonstrated that his stellar qualities were not confined to the playing fields. At a bonfire rally, while the team was being introduced, an over-excited yell leader cried, "And here's our world famous guard, Bob Mathias!"

A volley of mixed laughter and boos greeted the error, but Bob gallantly stepped to the embarrassed yell leader's rescue. When the noise subsided, he remarked, "The way I'm hitting the line lately Coach Chuck Taylor has probably been thinking of moving me to guard and letting Norm Manoogian [top Stanford guard] carry the ball." The good natured laughter that followed meant that the miscue had been forgiven.

Against relaxed and fired-up California, which under the rules could not return to the Rose Bowl and which had been eliminated from the title contest by losses to USC and UCLA, Stanford's football fortunes began to wane. The Bears won easily, 20-7, but it did not affect the Cards' Rose Bowl invitation. Against the withering charge of the California line, Mathias, though bothered somewhat by his injury, still was the most effective Indian ground gainer, averaging almost four yards per carry.

181

Before the Rose Bowl game with Illinois, Bob hurt his ankle. It worried Coach Taylor more than it did the Stanford fullback, even though it was to limit severely Bob's usefulness. On the eve of the tilt Taylor, who at thirty-one was the youngest coach ever to win a PCC title, was nervously biting his finger nails when Mathias strolled unconcernedly by. Looking at him, Taylor commented to an aide: "If I'm going to last long in this business, I'm going to have to learn how Bob does it."

Because of his injury, Mathias proved of little use to Stanford in the New Year's Day classic. He caught one long pass in the first half and Stanford led at the midway point, 7-6; but an Illinois pass interception changed the complexion of the game in the third quarter and the Indians came apart under the onslaught of the rugged Illini, 40-7.

With the advantage of hindsight, some experts declared that Stanford should never have gotten as far as it did. Whichever way the season was interpreted, it could not but be a tribute to the green Mathias. The spark of leadership he had provided seemed the telling factor in leading the largely veteran Indians to the conference championship before they became jaded or the breaks of combat began to turn against them.

For a lad who had not touched a football in competition for two years and was slowed by injuries, Mathias' regular season showing was remarkable: 397 yards in 95 rushes for an average of more than 4.2 yards per try, and eight touchdowns. Add to this his delivery of needed yardage in the pinches and pass receiving, blocking, and timely tackling.

Brief as his football career at "The Farm" has been, he already has joined Stanford's gridiron immortals. Many rate him the school's best fullback since Ernie Nevers. That would make him better than Bobby Grayson, the gifted line smacker of the "Vow Boys," who went to the Rose Bowl thrice in a row in the mid-thirties. Grayson himself admits it.

"If Mathias isn't as fast as I like to think I was," says Grayson, "he's more powerful. What's more, he's a terrific competitor, the kind that comes along only once in a generation. He showed his guts when he was seventeen and won the Olympic decathlon. Any other kid of his age would have been scared stiff. But not Mathias.

"When I saw him against Washington he showed his competitive heart at a time when he was pretty new in college football. He was, I thought, green and unpolished, but in the clutch he was great. Yes, he's a real life Rover Boy, if I ever saw one."

Chapter 9

THE CHAMP TRAINS

THE END OF FOOTBALL SEASON MEANT THE START OF another Olympic year for Bob Mathias. After a fling at skiing and basketball, in which he played five games for Phi Gamma Delta and gave his fraternity a big shove toward the Stanford intramural championship, Bob was ready to start serious training for the defense of his world decathlon crown.

In the interim, he was not neglecting his main purpose at the university—getting an education. He often had expressed his regret that sports and other activities took so much time away from his studies. Necessary lab work he arranged in morning periods. Finally, he moved out of the fraternity to an apartment without a telephone, so that he could have more privacy.

He made the change not only for academic reasons, but because by now he was more solidly than ever at the top of every Stanford co-ed's most eligible list. The phone at the Fiji house used to buzz regularly with feminine voices seeking Bob's company.

The following conversation, overheard on the campus and reported by Walt Gamage, *Palo Alto Times* sports editor, is a perfect illustration of how Bob ranks with the opposite sex:

Guy: "Hi, how about a date tonight?"

Gal: "Say, where do you get off trying to book me on such short notice? Just who do you think you are, anyway, Bob Mathias?"

But Bob continued to do very little dating. He went only to an occasional dance and he had no steady girl friend. Although he had given up on a medical career, he was just as serious about his new major, general education. He studied hard. He especially liked his science courses. His application eventually brought him the satisfaction of a "B" average, a very good record in view of Stanford's high scholastic rating.

Bob's sincerity, friendliness, modesty, steady good humor, and polite unaggressive manner are what make a hit with the distaff, more than his breakfast-food-ad build. In the be-bop slang of the co-eds he's "real George." One of his friends, the shapely swimming champion Sharon Geary, speaks for most of the campus when she says: "What I like about Bob is that he's a somebody who thinks he's a nobody. He just genuinely likes people."

Bob was now spinning about the campus in a new convertible his folks had given him. He was no spoiled rich man's son, however, and immediately took a job as campus representative of a clothing firm to help meet the increased expenses.

Then he was immersed in the long, lonesome conditioning grind that every trackman knows, especially a many-sided gem like Mathias. It was, of course, impossible for him to devote an equal amount of practice time to each of the ten events. Consequently he worked to improve himself in the ones in which he was weakest, and slighted his acknowledged specialties and favorites, such as the discus. Bob was faced with a new challenge at the start of the 1952 track season in the form of a revised international decathlon scoring chart that gave more points to running, in which the Europeans are stronger.

There were no complaints out of the defending titlist. He welcomed the toughening of the course and merely decided to try to improve himself in the cinder events during the regular campaign. This was the only concession he would make to his decathlon preparations.

When practice began, Coach Jack Weiershauser drew him aside and said: "Bob, we don't want to do anything to interfere with your Olympic plans. Just work out on what you please."

"No, coach," Bob answered, shying away from special treatment. "I'd rather do like the rest—compete wherever you need me."

Because of the muscle twinge in his back that had hampered him the year before, Bob took it easy getting back into his varied repertoire. He had only three weeks of work behind him when he went into the first dual meet and he waited until two days before to try his first flight of high hurdles. That was the test of whether he had completely shaken the old ailment. When he turned in a fair timing of 14.9 seconds his coaches exchanged relieved glances.

In the meet itself he entered four events, won three and took a third in the other. "It's the old Mathias," the fans told each other. In the high hurdle race he knocked down one of the barriers, but still won in the good time of 14.7. After, Weiershauser said: "He looked better than ever in the hurdles, especially near the finish where he had a tendency to get jerky. His time was really amazing for what little work he had done."

Bob even offered to work harder. "I'll run on the relay team if you want, Coach," Mathias told Weiershauser. But the mentor shook his head and smilingly refused. Aside he said, "I've never seen a boy who has done so much who regards himself so lightly."

During most of the dual meet season he heaved the discus between 150 and 160 feet, put the shot around 50 feet and stepped the 220-yard low hurdles around 23.6 seconds.

In the Big Meet with California the Bears would have upset the Indians except for one entrant who won both hurdle races, the discus, had cleared 13 feet in the pole vault and was ready to go higher when word came that Stanford had cinched it and he dropped out. Sound familiar?

"Every time we'd look like drawing even," a Cal official stated, "Mathias would come along with an armful of points and cool us. I've seen more exciting athletes, but never a better one. His consistency is absolutely unbelievable."

No one any longer questioned, "Can Bob do it?" But

a growing audience was wondering, "How does Bob do it?"

Most of the answer could be found by looking in on a typical Mathias day. During school Bob rises at seven o'clock in time to make an eight o'clock class. He breakfasts on orange juice, apple sauce, cereal, milk, eggs and bacon and sometimes hotcakes. For lunch he has something light, such as ham sandwiches, milk and ice cream. He eats nothing between meals and during training consumes few, if any, soft drinks, and of course no tobacco or liquor. He works out at the track—or on the football field—from three to five or six o'clock every day. After his workout he showers and dresses, then falls to a typical supper of roast beef, peas and carrots, salad (minus tomatoes), milk and ice cream.

After supper he plays the piano for a while or reads the sports pages or books his mother—she is a member of a book club—sends along. He studies for a couple of hours, then curls up in bed about ten o'clock. While school is on he still manages to get seven or eight hours of sleep at night, even when class assignments pile up.

Before a meet, because of all the events in which he competes, he has an eating problem that the one or two-event specialists don't face.

"At training table before a meet," Bob relates, "you'll see the sprinters drinking a glass of broth and the weight men stuffing themselves with steak. I've got to eat something in between."

Whether in competition or not, Bob sticks to the balanced diet he has followed for so long, knows so well, and values so highly. He likes plain, wholesome

189

foods. He dotes on meats, especially beef, which he takes in any form, steaks, roasts or hamburgers. He cannot get enough milk and ice cream. He likes plain, buttered vegetables. He shuns all highly spiced or seasoned foods.

Bob's likes and dislikes are such an important matter with legions of youngsters that it is fortunate his simple tastes do not have to be invented.

One day, while Bob was away at Stanford, Mrs. Mathias got a telephone call from one of her young Tulare neighbors.

"Hello, Mrs. Mathias," the boy said, "could you please tell me if Bob eats mayonnaise?"

A little taken aback, Mrs. Mathias answered, "No, not much. He likes a little on sandwiches but none on salads. Why?"

"Well," the boy said, "my mother is trying to make me eat it on salad and I don't like it and I just knew Bob didn't eat it either, but my mom said she just knew Bob did eat it to get as strong as he is, so I phoned you. Thanks, Mrs. Mathias." And he hung up.

When school is out and he is concentrating on getting ready for a decathlon, Mathias alters his schedule slightly. He goes to bed around eleven o'clock and sets the alarm for nine A.M. If he wakes up before, he simply goes back to sleep until the alarm rings. He loafs till ten, eats a hearty breakfast, then skips lunch.

He works out from three to five, on events in the sequence in which they occur in a two-day decathlon meet. One day, after loosening up, he'll run the 100 meters a couple of times, then work on getting his step

190

in the broad jump, then spend some time in the shot put ring, from there proceed to the high jump pit and finally run a 220 or modified 440 to keep in trim for the 400 meters.

The next afternoon he'll practice, in order, the high hurdles, discus, pole vault and javelin. He never rehearses a 1500 meter race as such. He'll jog a couple of laps or, as when his brother Jimmy joined him at Stanford to prepare for the national decathlon meet, he will run for about ten minutes at a stretch over the campus golf course to develop wind for the longer race and get his system used to the change. During the 1952 dual meet season Bob also tried a couple of regular 880's, roughly equal to half of a metric mile.

Bob admits that within this rigorous schedule he is often tempted to neglect certain events, but the presence of his coaches, Weiershauser and Dean, is a deterrent. "If it weren't for them I'd often skip the 100," Bob says. "It's hard work and if they weren't around I probably wouldn't do it." The coaches also go over with Mathias slow motion pictures of his form, painstakingly searching out weak spots and suggesting corrections.

After the 1952 dual meet season a series of attractions drawing the top track and field talent in the country served as excellent means of keeping Bob sharp for the combined national decathlon championships and Olympic tryout in July at Tulare.

One of these, the NCAA meet at Berkeley, California, in late June, doubled as an elimination test for the Olympic tryouts in individual events. Mathias qualified three times with a second in the high hurdles, a sixth in the discus and a seventh in the shot put. Only six places counted for the Olympic trial, but in the shot put, Bob was edged by a foreign student from the University of Michigan who was ineligible for the U. S. team.

Bob didn't care much if he made the Olympic squad in an individual event in addition to the decathlon and again demonstrated his enviable ability to relax. The night before he and Gene left Tulare to drive to Los Angeles, site of the trials, Gene was nervous and couldn't sleep. Bob sawed off his usual nine hours. They reached Los Angeles at eleven A.M. and, as there were still two hours before the meet, they took a hotel room. Bob yawned and said, "Gene, wake me up at 12:15, I'm going to take a nap." He immediately fell asleep again.

In the competition itself, Mathias didn't do much, but the rivalry for places on the Olympic team was so intense that he had nothing to be ashamed of. Bob was fifth in his heat of the high hurdles, running 14.8 seconds; eighth in the discus with a throw of better than 161 feet. This event was won by his fellow Tularean, Sim Iness, who approached 175 feet. And in the shot put he was last in a field of eleven with only 48 feet, 9 inches. The latter event was termed the greatest competitive shot put of all time, by no less an authority than Cordner Nelson, editor of *Track and Field News*. There were 51 puts over 55 feet and the third and fourth place men had the longest marks in history for such low finishes.

With that stiff, three-event tune-up behind him, Mathias was ready for his first crack at a decathlon in two years. He was on the spot. After such a long lay-off could he come back to recapture the national title he had relinquished by default in 1951?

Just prior to the two-day carnival, for which Tulare again adopted a festive air, Bob grew somewhat irritable and this was interpreted by Coach Weiershauser as a good sign. "That means his condition is razor keen," Weiershauser explained. Bob's father, who had observed him in action ever since he first drew on a school uniform agreed. "Just before a meet that's the way Bob acts—snappy. He should do all right."

On the nights of July 1 and 2, 1952, before 6,000 joyous hometown fans Bob more than vindicated that prediction. He got enough competition to make it the finest decathlon affair in history and Mr. Decathlon put on a show that will long remain in the memory of those who saw it.

He bettered his own world record by amassing 7,825 points. His previous record—8,042, according to the old scoring system—was only 7,444 points under the system now in vogue.

He improved on nine of the ten marks he made when setting the old standard and in eight of the ten events he recorded his finest performances of any decathlon. Usually strongest in the second five events, Bob showed so much improvement in the first five events of the program that he replaced Bill Albans as the greatest first-day man in decathlon history, with a score of 4,394 points to Albans' 4,385, made in 1950. He also became the only one ever to gain four AAU decathlon titles.

Mathias opened strong with a 10.8 seconds 100 meters, reached 23 feet, 5¼ inches with only two broad jumps, then ran into trouble in the shot put. On his first two heaves he failed to better 47 feet. But on his third try Mathias again found that extra something and pushed the iron ball 49 feet, 10⅝ inches, more than two feet better than he ever had done in the ten-eventer.

In the high jump Bob didn't touch the bar on any of his jumps, and when he got over the height of 6 feet, 2¾ inches with more than an inch of air showing, he quit to conserve his strength.

The 400 meters race between Mathias and Milt Campbell, the surprisingly adept Negro prepster from New Jersey, was a pulse-stopper. Campbell had the pole position, Mathias the outside lane. At the gun Bob dug for the inside position, but he couldn't take it away from the game colored lad and the pair fought shoulder to shoulder for 300 yards. Both were spent from the effort and as they turned into the back stretch they were both wavering. Neither would quit, however, and Campbell won by two feet as the crowd loudly applauded them both.

Campbell had extended himself so much that he was sick most of the night, but he came back the next evening for another great effort, pushing Bob, who fell slightly off his first night's pace, to the new record.

Mathias nicked three hurdles but turned in a good time of 14.6 seconds. In the discus he was way short of his best at 157 feet, 11⅝ inches, but it still was superb for the decathlon. Then Bob came to the pole vault and faltered. In every event hitherto he had bettered his previous decathlon best. Now he missed twice at 12 feet, 3¾ inches before calmly collecting himself and soaring over the height. But he could get no higher.

Coming to the javelin, Mathias needed a throw of better than 180 feet to shatter his previous point record. He approached that on his first toss, but he had stepped over the foul line. On his second attempt he was more careful in his step and with a spring-like snap of his supple right arm sent the spear hurtling 193 feet, 10⅝ inches. That nabbed him his world's record and Bob padded it with a clocking of 4:55.3 in the 1,500 meters, only one-tenth of a second off his all-time best.

Campbell, inexperienced in many events, still had enough innate ability to finish second with 7,055 points, remarkable for a lad in his first decathlon. Floyd Simmons, with 6,804 points, qualified for the third spot on the Olympic team, as he had in 1948. Bill Albans was pressing him until he dropped out with an injured wrist.

Like other Tulareans, the Mathiases practically held open house for the decathlon entrants. One evening at the dinner table one of their guests, Phil Mulkey, of Purdy, Missouri, recounted a moving story. Casting an awe struck look around, Phil said: "You know, four years ago back in Missouri, when I heard what Bob did at London while he was just out of high school, I made up my mind to try to be just like him. I trained long and hard. I only finished seventeenth in the point standings here, but, gosh, here I am eating at the very same table with the whole Mathias family."

On that inspirational note, Bob set off for Helsinki and the unprecedented effort to win two world's iron-man titles in a row.

Chapter 10

HISTORY AT HELSINKI

Bob Mathias approached the fifteenth modern Olympic Games in Helsinki, Finland, in the summer of 1952 with an air of quiet confidence.

Since he had rocked the sports world by winning the Olympic decathlon in London, Bob had become a man. Now, at twenty-one, he stood six feet, three inches tall and weighed 199 pounds, a gain of three inches and twelve pounds since the 1948 Games.

In the intervening years he had improved on virtually all the marks he had made at London. Also behind him was a rugged season of football, in which he had led Stanford to the Rose Bowl.

Tulareans, too, were quietly confident. They had come to regard their Bob as a super athlete, for whom victory was preordained. But they still hadn't completely recovered from the uneasiness which gripped them early in the 1952 Olympic year.

Bob already had opened his spring workouts at Stanford when news reached both him and Tulare that, for some inexplicable reason, the decathlon scoring system had been changed. The new standard, created by the International Amateur Athletic Federation at a convention in Brussels in the fall of 1951, provided extra points for the running events and deducted points for field events.

It seemed as if the scoring method had been changed to handicap the Tulare Titan.

And all Tulare was stunned. Quickly the townsfolk went to work with their pencils and found that the world record of 8,042 points, which Bob had set in the 1950 Nationals, shrank to 7,443 when figured on the new table.

While the rest of the nation was occupied with talk of whether Dwight Eisenhower would return to seek the Republican presidential nomination, the good citizens of Tulare were discussing over their back fences the seemingly discriminatory action against their Bob. At first, there was talk of a protest, but they did not know where to lodge it.

Bob himself took the news in stride. Like every other red-blooded American boy, he dotes on competition. The tougher it is, the better he likes it. He still had plenty of time, he figured, to concentrate on the running events, which now paid higher dividends. And he would pay less attention to his best events, the weights, which counted less in the new order. The discus, of course, always had been his pet event.

All spring he worked hard on the running events and, by the time of the NCAA meet in Berkeley, Calif., he barreled off the starting blocks like a bona fide sprinter. And there were few finer hurdlers in the land. Bob had grown and hardened into the acme of manhood, and felt that he was ready for the already torturing decathlon, which had toughened with him.

Mathias was by far the most popular athlete among those of sixty-seven nations who gathered in Helsinki for the 1952 Games. Clean-cut, handsome and ideally proportioned, he easily was recognized on the streets of the Finnish metropolis in his blue Olympic blazer, grey slacks and gabardine hat after his picture had appeared in the papers. In fact, he was regarded by the young Finns as the living, walking, talking embodiment of the Olympic ideal.

Strolling down the Mannerheimintie, Helsinki's main stem, several days before the decathlon opened, Bob was stopped by two youths who recognized him. As they shook his hand, a crowd quickly formed. Youngsters frisked their pockets for paper which Bob could autograph. "Sign pliss," they pleaded. A pretty little girl of about twelve, whose golden hair hung in pigtails, caught sight of the center of the attraction as she came out of a nearby pastry shop. Hurriedly she rushed back into the store and reappeared a few seconds later carrying an unwrapped small chocolate cake. Trying to jockey her way through the fans to present it to Bob, she dropped the cake from her upheld hand. Embarrassed, she didn't know whether to laugh or cry.

"Never mind," comforted Bob, as he patted her shoulder, "I couldn't have eaten it anyway. It's against training regulations. But I appreciate it just the same."

A wonderful smile illuminated the little girl's face.

199

She seemed to understand what the big American hero was saying, even though she spoke no English.

Most of the autograph-seeking younger fry operated in polite little pressure groups. After obtaining a signature, the boys would salute the athlete and the girls would curtsey. In the exchange mart, a Bob Mathias autograph was worth at least ten of the others, unless the collection included the name of Emil Zatopek, the Czechoslovakian army major, who was to help the Yankees rewrite the Olympic record book by winning the marathon, 5,000 meters and 10,000 meters.

Although the Finnish kids don't know it, many of their Mathias autographs, taken before the Games opened, are counterfeit. Several other American athletes were not so obliging as Bob, and they developed a little trick to save them time on their shopping tours. When apprehended by a crowd of moppets, they'd merely point to another athlete and exclaim:

"Mathias? There's Mathias!"

If the surprised fellow happened to be an American, the youngsters usually got their Bob Mathias signature, forgery though it was.

Later, however, the youths became acquainted with Mathias' handsome face, and the deception was of scant use.

Reporters from all over the world came to the American camp to question Coach Brutus Hamilton about his one-man track team. Hamilton, who is both track coach and athletic director at the University of California, told the newsmen that Bob was "American youth at its very best."

"Like all boys," continued Hamilton, "Bob likes to have fun, but he's always dignified and never makes a false step. There's a halo 'round his head, I tell you. But I'm thankful, I guess, that all my trackmen aren't like him. If they were, I'd have nothing to do."

One reporter who had made the boat trip with the 1948 American Olympic squad remembered how cheerful Bob was on the junket.

When a card game was breaking up and the athletes were showing signs either of seasickness or homesickness, Bob stepped to a nearby piano and gave with the boogie-woogie. The fellows promptly snapped out of it and soon were around the piano singing to Bob's accompaniment. Later, when bedtime approached, Bob was heard playing dreamy waltzes. This was during the latter part of the voyage. For the first two nights, Mathias himself was looking green.

Now, at Helsinki, Bob was kept so busy answering reporters' questions and signing autographs, he had little time for his favorite hobby of photography. He took but one roll of film until after the decathlon was over. But he more than made up for it later, both at Helsinki and in the post-Olympic tour, through the major European countries.

Young America always has been known for its friendliness, and this quality is most pronounced in Bob. So it was not surprising that he twice visited the Russian camp before the Helsinki decathlon.

In politics and business, vindictiveness is common, but most athletes, especially great ones like Mathias, forgive as readily as young children, and here again Bob had a chance to prove it.

After Mathias' confounding conquest at London, the Soviet radio had ranted that he was a spoiled, exploited youth. The announcer also called Bob a bum, boasting that in Esthonia there was an athlete (Heino Lipp) who could mop up the field with the American schoolboy. (The Soviet Union had sat out the London Games.)

If Mathias even remembered the tirade, it meant nothing to him now. He was eager to see what the Russian athletes really were like and they, it developed, were just as anxious to look over the American Wonder Man.

When Bob's destination was learned after he had departed for the Russian village, several athletes and officials were somewhat concerned. After all, the strained relations between the two countries couldn't be denied, and there were expressions of fear as to Mathias' safety.

Bob had been invited by one of the Russians he had met at a workout to drop in at the Soviet camp at Otaniemi. To Mathias, it was just like calling on friends, and he was both curious and happy over the invitation.

As he approached the gate of the little Iron Curtain village, six miles from the stadium, he was recognized by two big Russians in blue sweat suits, who broke into wide smiles and came forward to welcome him. Other Soviet athletes joined the huddle. Some of them spoke faltering English, and thoughts were exchanged without too much difficulty.

When Bob offered them chewing gum, the Russians eyed it skeptically.

Mathias quickly unwrapped a stick and stuck it in his mouth. "Juicy Fruit," he said. "Good."

One of the Russians sniffed his piece before unwrapping it, but soon all the Russians were chewing away like Americans at a baseball game.

In exchange, the Soviets gave Bob cigarettes, kopeks and bottles of cognac. Bob accepted the gifts graciously, even though he couldn't use the tobacco and liquor.

On his tour of the camp, Mathias was taken to an expansive hall decorated with Russian flags. On one hung color paintings of Stalin, Molotov, and members of the Politburo. In one corner was a display of huge cakes, reserved for the gold medal winners. (Of these, the USSR already had won plenty in almost all sports but track, the one sport in which they had an all-consuming desire to excel.)

Preparations were being made now for the evening meal, and on the table were caviar, vegetables, tomato salad, fish and cheese. The Russians brought in all their food and drink daily from Leningrad. One-inch steaks, along with potatoes and peas, were to follow. Waiters in full dress were pouring two glasses of cognac and vodka for each plate. Mathias assumed the table was for the some three hundred stern-faced officials who accompanied the Soviet squad.

The atmosphere at Otaniemi was anything but grim. In fact, Mathias realized at once that the Russians were more comfortably established than the athletes of the Western world. Here the furniture was neatly upholstered, the floors carpeted, and he also liked the permanent dining hall, the indoor running track and gym. In contrast, the Western camp at Kapylae had concrete floors and plain beds and stools. Moreover, meals were served in a cold, drafty room.

Neither did the Iron Curtain competitors lack for entertainment. Folk dancers, ballet companies, actors and singers from virtually every province appeared in endless relays to entertain the athletes.

Bob asked a few of his Soviet friends to visit him, but they only shook their heads sadly.

"It's against regulations," they made the American athletic ambassador understand.

Returning to the American quarters, Bob told newsmen that the Soviets, as individuals, were just like anybody else.

"If they weren't wearing red jerseys," went on Mathias, "I couldn't have told them from the athletes of other countries. They have the same desires and emotions as our athletes, and they behave just as we do in victory and defeat.

"They're good athletes, all right. They've already proved that. I feel that competing against other nations is a fine thing for them. They're finding out that we're not so bad after all, and we're learning the same thing about them."

Much more at ease in interviews now, Bob felt in an expansive mood and he continued:

"They've been fair and square in all the events I've seen them in, and they seem to enjoy the competition as genuinely as we do.

"The idea of the Olympic Games is to foster international good will and sportsmanship. That has been accomplished here. After all, the Games are contests between individuals and not nations. So it's up to us competitors to form friendships."

At no time before the decathlon opened did Mathias show a suggestion of tenseness. Most of his spare time he put in sleeping, much to the consternation of his teammates. They couldn't sit still for five minutes, let alone fall asleep in the brightness of the Land of the Midnight Sun.

The University of California is Stanford's bitter rival, but at Helsinki Bob found Cal men aligned with him. In addition to Coach Hamilton, he was administered to by Bob Peterson, a trainer from the UC. And among those who covered his every movement were Bob Rubin and Lefty Stern, sports publicists at the sprawling Berkeley university. Also available for advice, in a non-official capacity, was Jack Weiershauser, his Stanford track coach.

Remembering Bob's travail at London, which included the huddling for hours under a blanket in the rain, Hamilton had his staff take mattresses to the Helsinki stadium for Mathias and the other American decathloners to relax on between events.

Mathias took it easy around the Olympic Village the day before the decathlon opened. Mail now was begining to reach the American hero from all parts of the world, and he had time to read the letters which required no translating. Among the epistles was one from

205

President Wallace Sterling of Stanford, telling him that the whole school was behind him.

Bob was pleased also to hear from the leader of a team he subsequently was to be a part of, a team greater than the Stanford Rose Bowl eleven or the American Olympic team, which was to win the championship of the entire Helsinki Games. This was the U.S. Marine Corps, and the letter was from General Lemuel Shepherd, who wrote that the Corps extended him the best of luck.

The young man winced perceptively when he came to the last paragraph of a letter from his mother.

"Please remember to write," she admonished.

For all his virtues, Bob is no absolute paragon. Among his weaknesses, and one which he shares with so many, is a distaste for correspondence. Much of the negligence stems from his dislike of talking about himself.

The medical practice of his father had increased yearly, and the good doctor felt that he could ill afford to spare the time for the trip to Helsinki. Both his mother and father had watched Bob's conquest at London. But Bob was not without family support. Brother Jimmy, who also had cheered Bob at London, made the flight to Helsinki with a group of University of Southern California students. He was to enter Occidental College, near Los Angeles, in September.

Ominous dark clouds hung low over Helsinki as the eagerly awaited decathlon got under way at ten o'clock on Friday, July 25, 1952. A stiff wind whipped persistently across the red brick track.

A large crowd was on hand and more youngsters than

in the previous days were noted in the throng, their imagination fired by the first appearance of the great athlete from America, whom some newspapers were calling Mr. Superman.

Could he retain his title against the onslaught of the Russians, who for the past five years had been training with a fervor unknown in the Democracies? True, Heino Lipp, who long had been touted by the Soviets as the world's greatest decathlon man, was not entered. But this could have meant that he had been surpassed by Vladimir Volkov, Sergei Kuznetsov and other younger all-arounders. Some writers said that Lipp had been kept home for political reasons, but, if this were the case, Mathias had the good tact not to ask about it on his visit at the USSR camp.

However, the biggest threat to Mathias, the European press conceded, was France's towering Ignace Heinrich, who had come in second to Bob in the 1948 Games. It was written that Heinrich had "improved tremendously" and that Mathias would have to score more than 8,000 points to beat him.

But Bob saw little to fear in Heinrich. The pair worked out together in the Olympic camp, and Mathias noted that the six-foot four-inch Frenchman virtually knocked himself out every time he vaulted.

While Mathias made friends with scores of foreign athletes who sought him out, his closest chum was the genial Heinrich. Ignace spoke a little English, but most of their conversation was in French. Bob had had two years of the language at Stanford.

207

"*Très bien*," you could hear them tell each other after a workout.

Mathias also found time to coach Milton Campbell, the genial Negro youngster, who had given him such stiff competition in the combined American decathlon championships and Olympic trials a few weeks before at Tulare.

The night before the Helsinki decathlon opened, Bob told Campbell: "Now go to bed early, Milty. You're going to need lots of rest to be in shape for the 1,500 meters [closing event of the two-day grind]."

"Shucks, Bob," joshed Campbell, "I'm going to make so many points in the first nine events I'll be able to sit out the long one."

Mathias, whose favorite event certainly is not the 1,500 meters, smiled: "I know how you feel, Milty. Might do the same thing myself."

The close relationship between this pair, one a well-to-do doctor's son and the other a member of a struggling minority, was a revelation to the entrants from the Communist countries, which harp so much on discrimination in America. Bob's early training to respect individuals no matter from what race, creed or color was clearly shown in his respect for Milton Campbell.

Now, as the field of twenty-eight assembled for final instructions, Bob felt a little sad that his old friend from the 1948 Games, Enrique Kistermacher, was not among the starters. It was Kistermacher, an Army officer, who unwittingly had helped Mathias to a super-performance at London with his ridicule of the seventeen-year-old kid. It had only served as a spur for the unknown boy from the unknown town.

Waiting for his turn in the opening event, the 100-meter dash, Mathias let his eye roam over the stadium as it pulsated with the cries of a score of tongues. He felt a slight butterfly in his stomach—"like before a funeral" he told a teammate—but it quickly passed. Outwardly he was the picture of relaxation.

Bob recalled how nervous he had been at the London Olympics. The decathlon then was a new event to him. He didn't know what to expect. A mere high school boy, he could have been made to look very foolish by the older men of other lands, but now he was the champ, the top dog.

"Mathias up," snapped the announcer. Focus of all eyes, he paid no heed to the crowd that gathered around him as he took the on your mark order.

As he knelt into take off position, Bob reminded himself how necessary it was to post a fast time, for more points now were awarded in the sprints. "Then, too," went on his conscience, "you must get off in front in this decathlon. This competition is even tougher than before, fellow, and you'd better show 'em who's boss early."

There was a click and Bob was off as if jet-propelled. As he straightened up, he noticed that the two others in his heat, Germany's Sepp Hipp and Portugal's De Matos Fernandes, weren't running. Embarrassed, he realized he had mistaken the loud click of a movie camera grinding away near him for the starting gun.

Now he could take no chance, for two false starts in

209

an Olympic decathlon event mean disqualification. So Bob sat back on his haunches to await the gun. Once he got it for sure, he was away like a runaway express. Because of the slow take off, he could do no better than 10.9, a tenth of a second off his Tulare tryout time. Yet he finished seven yards in front of Hipp, but his time was well under the Russian pair of Volkov and Kuznetsov who, as if synchronized, were both caught in 11.4.

Determination welled up in Mathias' throat as he made ready for the broad jump, one of his better events. Charging down the runway, he took off cleanly, but the man with the tape called it 6.95 meters. This would be 22 feet, 9.72 inches. (With the greatest Olympic field ever assembled, everyone now paid much more attention to the fine shadings of the metric measuring system.) Bob shook his head in dismay. He had done 23 feet, 5¼ inches when he set the world record of 7,815 points in the tryouts.

On his second try he improved his mark only slightly —to 22 feet, 10.80 inches. Kicking hard on his last attempt, Mathias felt a stab of pain in his left thigh as he came down. It was a poor jump, and he lay in the sand for a moment rubbing his thigh. For a second a black whirlpool of distress swept through his mind. Did this mean the end of the 1952 Olympics for him? Could he possibly go on through the gruelling afternoon the next day? "Certainly," Bob told himself as he cheerfully picked himself up.

Still seemingly synchronized, the Soviet pair turned in identical distances of 23 feet, 3.12 inches for 818 points.

Bob's mediocre first leap was his best, but it was good for only 779 points. He was trailing and, worse yet, he was slightly hobbled by this thigh injury.

Huzzahs now broke out in the Soviet section of the stands. So this was the All-American Boy? Had he seriously expected to dominate the Russians, too? Ah, this time the lad was in over his head!

Gloom as dark as the skies gripped the American and Finnish throngs. Had Bob really met his match? Intently, the crowd edged forward to catch his reactions, his stride. Was he hurt? Could he go on?

An American youngster broke from the tiers of spectators. Waving his score card, he headed for the field shouting: "Come on, Bob. Let's show 'em." Before he reached the track, however, he was intercepted by stadium police who hauled him back to his seat.

Then came a break for Mathias, who trailed the leader, Campbell, by ten points. There was time to return to the village for lunch, and Bob was able to secure a thick juicy steak to fortify himself for the long cold afternoon ahead. He seemed utterly unmoved by the turn of events.

Some athletes are what is known as front-runners. They're great only when ahead. Mathias learned early to thrive on adversity. He usually won the hard way, coming from behind after a slow start. His thigh bothered him only a little now, and he felt in his heart he could come back strong.

As he re-entered the stadium, Bob was engulfed by a gang of kids, and he remained to give each one his autograph.

211

"What do you think of Mathias' chances now?" a Finnish sports writer asked Hamilton. "Will he come back?"

"Yes, of course," replied the coach. "Bob not only is the greatest athlete in the world but he's also the greatest competitor. You watch him now. When the pressure's on, he's at his best."

As Hamilton spoke other athletes were pacing nervously about the infield, dragging their toes and talking first to one competitor then another. Conversely, Bob was curled up on the sidelines in a blanket, looking as relaxed as a New Mexico Indian under a warm spring sun. He again was putting to good use the lesson he had learned long ago of the value of relaxation between events. By now his scientific approach to track permitted him total relaxation. He knew he had only to deal with two inanimate forces: gravity and time.

Often Bob falls asleep as he dozes between events, but there was no time now, for his number was up at the shot put circle. Stripping off his sweat jersey, he revealed the back and shoulders of a gymnast. Every one of his rippling muscles went into action in a thrust of unbridled power. The iron ball traveled 50 feet, 2.37 inches, and Mathias was in front of the decathlon field, never again to be headed. None of the other competitors could crack the 50-foot mark.

Like a chess player, Bob had learned to look ahead and, like a boxer, he had discovered how to conserve his strength. Even as a high school boy at the London Olympics, he had refused to take his turn at the pole vault until the bar was set at ten feet. He saw no reason for squandering his energy on heights he knew he could clear. Now, still uncertain of the pinched nerve in his thigh, he pulled out of the high jump after having reached 6 feet, 2.81 inches. But first he had studied his brown decathlon book to make sure he had sufficient points.

It took hours for the big field to complete an event and Bob had considerable spare time. Since the raw wind, whipping down from the Arctic Ocean, had increased in velocity, he spent most of his extra time on a mattress in a room under the stands. Sleep came easily.

He reappeared early in the evening in a heavy overcoat, supplemented by a blanket.

It was nearly eight o'clock when Mathias' 400-meter heat came up. He tried a couple of short warm-up dashes, and the leg felt satisfactory enough for him to decide to open wide the throttle in this, the final event of the day. Blazing down the slightly wet track in an all out effort, he was caught in 22.5 seconds for the first 200 meters. In comparison, Jamaica's George Rhoden, who a few hours earlier had broken the 400-meter dash record with a 45.9, traveled only a little faster than Bob's pace for the half-way mark. The big boy then hung on gamely to post a 50.2, fastest time of his young life.

Trudging back past the stands, Bob was hailed by his brother Jimmy.

"That was terrific, Bob," shouted Jimmy. "Worth 828 points. That's forty-two more than you got in the Tulare trials."

Bob realized that his concentration on the running events had paid off, but he could only say:

"Gosh, Jimmy, I've never been so tired in my life. I doubt if those extra points are worth it."

Shortly after, Bob had caught his breath, and he decided things weren't so tough after all. On his way to the showers he kept throwing his ailing leg in the air as if he were hurdling.

"It feels okay," he told reporters. "I should be in good shape tomorrow."

With 4,367 points, he was just twenty-seven off his first day's pace at the Tulare tryouts, in which he set a world's record of 7,825.

And the Russian threat had been completely dispelled. Volkov was in seventh place and Kuznetsov in twelfth. His teammates, Campbell and Simmons, followed Mathias.

Bob hit the sack as soon as he returned to the Olympic Village. As is his habit, he arose at seven o'clock the next morning. It seemed then that he had never seen a more dismal day since London. The threatening storm clouds still oppressed Helsinki and, worse yet, there was a slight pain in his left thigh. He took a short walk around his room, flexing his leg in hurdle action. Then, as was now his custom, Mathias went back to bed for a short nap. No use worrying about it, he reasoned.

Awakened an hour later, he quickly slipped into his uniform, which bore the now famous No. 1039, and was off at once for the stadium. His leg muscle had tightened overnight, and he wanted a rubdown and a heat treatment before starting the long final day's battle.

214

The head trainer, Eddie Wojecki of Rice Institute, thought he detected a trace of concern outlined in Mathias' usually placid face.

"I see you're still a partial red-head, Bob," kidded Wojecki, trying to relax him completely. He was eyeing the wisp of henna remaining in Mathias' brown hair from a dousing his Phi Gamma Delta brethren had given him during one of his deep mid-day naps near the end of the school year.

"I can't seem to get rid of it," replied Mathias. "Oh well, I ought to be able to sweat it out today."

An elastic bandage was placed on Bob's left thigh, and he was ready for the five remaining tests.

Bob had often been touched by the kind-heartedness of other nationalities, but nothing quite so moved him as an incident which occurred as he moved toward the track.

He was surrounded quickly by a group of Finns who, concerned over Mathias' opening-day performance, had decided to give him a helper. Then they presented their man—a little Finnish official with a warm smile. Bob never caught his name, and to this day he regrets that he never did learn it.

The helper's job was to follow Bob around the track with a score book to keep him posted on just how he stood in reference to the record.

Mathias had planned to bear down hard on the opening event—the 110-meter high hurdles—since he now was well rested. But, whenever he lifted his left foot for a hurdle, pain swept up his statuesque frame. He hit the first hurdle.

215

"Nothing must happen to me now," Bob told himself. "This means everything. I can't let anyone down."

Consciously, he never let down before the leg throbs, but now he tried to step up his pace even faster. He had hoped to hit his all-time best—14.2 seconds—but the slight deviation in form prevented it. In his anxiety he was over-running the hurdles. The clocking was 14.7.

But things weren't so bad as they seemed. When the other participants had completed their hurdles, the scoreboard showed that only young Campbell had bettered Bob's mark. Milt turned in a 14.5. They were the only two, in fact, to break 15 seconds.

And there was more encouraging news for Mathias, though he was sorry to hear it. Friend Ignace Heinrich, expected to be Bob's chief competition, dropped out after the first event of the day. He had suffered an ankle sprain and a back injury the opening day and found he could not go on.

A light rain had started to fall as the competitors made ready for the discus. It was a welcome event for Bob, for not only is it his best but also it would afford him the opportunity to rest his leg. He still was 179 points ahead of Campbell, in second place, but was running behind his world record pace.

After a long warm up, Mathias went into a powerful pin wheel from which he unloosed a throw of 153 feet, 10 inches. Bob rated among the world's very best discus men, and this toss, while good, was a disappointment to him.

Coach Hamilton thought it unfair that Mathias was

prevented by international rules from using his own discus.

"The boys," said Hamilton to an assistant, "should be allowed to use their own discus. Bob's got an old beaten up one that he likes a lot better than the official discus. It threw him off."

Even though Mathias had slumped slightly in the discus, he far surpassed the field. Campbell, next high, was 21 feet below Bob.

Mathias was in more real danger in the discus than he realized. One of the entrants lost control of a practice throw, and it narrowly missed Bob's head. He never saw it till he heard screams and looked up just as it spun harmlessly into the ground not far from him.

Other athletes headed at this time for the Olympic Village for lunch, but Bob remained at the stadium for a rubdown in preparation for the crucial event—the pole vault. Here it would be determined if he could crack his own world record; also if his thigh would stand further punishment.

The capricious rain was back as the decathlon field assembled for the most trying of all events. On and on went the vaulting, through sunshine and rain and chilling winds, for five hours and forty minutes. The javelin throw was supposed to start at 4:30 but it didn't until 8 P.M. For Bob, anxious to get it over with, it was a frustrating period of interminable waits, almost as bad as at London. When the rains came, he threw a towel over his head and covered his sweatsuit with a raincoat. When the sun shone he lay down and studied his decathlon book, with the aid of his Finnish friend, to de-

217

termine how high he would have to go to get back in the race for a new point record.

While the final events were taking place, Dink Templeton, the old Stanford track coach, came down on the field. Bob recognized him through the murky gloom and went up to him. "Here, Dink," he said, offering the old man his blanket, "get out of the rain." What other athlete would think of a friend in such a trying time as this!

To conserve his strength, Mathias didn't start vaulting until the bar reached 11 feet, 1.86 inches. On his first try he knocked off the bamboo as the throng groaned. But he threw himself cleanly over the next time. Instantly a din arose from the stands. He was using a glass pole invented by Coach Jackson to hold better a man of Mathias' weight.

As the bar inched upward, the pain in his leg increased. Each time he charged down the runway, his heart seemed to stand still. "Would this," he wondered, "be my last try?" But he fought back his fears and, encouraged by the cheers of "Let's go, Bob . . . Higher, Higher," he found himself getting over the bar in good form despite the ailing leg.

Finally, as if inspired by a sudden sunburst, Bob swung his heavy well-knit frame well over the bar, pushed back his pole and was clear at the amazing height of 13 feet, 1.16 inches. The vault was good for 745 points, 125 more than he collected in his record performance at Tulare. He now was ahead for the first time of his world record pace, ahead by 26 points.

After surveying the height, Bob pulled out his brown

218

book. He found the point yield sufficient to permit him to withdraw from the event at that height. There was no use antagonizing the leg more than necessary. Too, the pole vault always had been Bob's toughest event to master because of his size. His Finnish friend nodded agreement to the withdrawal plan. So, waving to the crazed crowd, he walked slowly into the dressing room for another rubdown.

The massage was beneficial to the sore leg, and it also served to rest the Californian for the final two events—the javelin throw and 1,500-meter run.

Hamilton came into the dressing room to see how his charge was making out. "Remember, Bob," the coach cautioned, "you can't afford to let up any in the javelin."

"Don't worry, Mr. Hamilton," replied Bob. "I'll get it way out there. I promise."

Before Bob could pick up his javelin after returning to the field, his Finnish friend called him to one side.

In broken English he explained that Bob could exceed his record of 7,825 points if he threw the spear 195 feet and ran 4:52 in the 1,500 meters.

Again the crowd scrambled to its feet to cheer as Mathias prepared for his first throw. He gave the shaft a mighty toss but it fell short. Something was wrong.

In the stands Jack Weiershauser, his Stanford coach, noted that Bob had neglected to follow through. Since Jack was there in an unofficial capacity, he could not enter the field to talk to Bob. Quickly he rounded up a gang of American rooters and sent the youths to the far stands near where Bob was tossing.

By the time they had arrived, Mathias had flubbed his second throw, too.

"Follow through, Bob," they yelled.

A volunteer cheerleader began waving his hands, gesturing to the crowd to join in. A chant was started:

> *Oh, Bob. Hey you.*
> *Don't forget to follow through.*

The Finns didn't understand but they were willing to help out anyway, and soon the whole stands echoed out the words "Follow through."

Mathias caught the message, and he smiled out his thanks. Then he recognized his coach. "I got you," he shouted.

Then in as perfect a pitch as the javelin-fond Finns have ever seen, he sent the lance whistling through the cold half light. Into the turf it dug, a distance of 195 feet, 3⅛ inches away, another all-time best. This put Mathias 28 points in front of the record pace. To set a new mark now he had only to traverse the body-wracking 1,500 meters under 4:55.3.

His damaged knee had not troubled him since the supper-hour rubdown, but Bob was not at all confident that it would hold up for the metric mile, his poorest event. A big fellow, he's just not built for it and, too, his boyhood anemia left him a trifle short of the endurance necessary for distance running. It's his only athletic deficiency.

A mile run is rough enough for a fresh athlete. These decathloners had gone into action at ten A.M., and it was now nearly ten P.M. Battered and weary, they drove themselves on. So wearisome was the ordeal that a durable Finn, Erkki Hautamaeki, collapsed near the finish line.

At the head of the stretch now, waiting the timer's gun, Mathias rubbed his tightly-taped thigh with both hands and then lifted his head aloft as if asking for divine aid. There was grim determination written on his face as he took off: Bob had promised himself that, come what would, he'd get home in 4:55.

For the first half of the race, he kept a moderate pace to be sure about his leg. Darkness had settled upon the stadium, and Bob would have been almost invisible were it not for the eerie cross illumination of the Olympic torch and the electric scoreboard which played on him as he ran. The ailing muscle throbbed with each contact with the ground, but the pain was not severe. Or so Bob told himself. At the halfway mark, certain that he could finish the race, Mathias stepped up his stride, and he roared across the finish line to a tumultuous ovation in 4:50.8.

The pulsating comeback in the face of pain and threatened exhaustion had brought Bob Mathias his second decathlon title, a feat no other man in history had achieved. And more than that, he had piled up 7,887 points in adverse weather to exceed by sixty-two digits his former record.

Among the first to grasp his hand was Coach Hamilton.

"I'm glad I didn't let you down, Mr. Hamilton."

"Bob," the kindly Brutus smiled through misty eyes, "you'll never let anyone down."

Mathias remained on the field to watch Campbell run his heat. "That's it, Milty," he called, "pour it on, kid."

The some 15,000 who remained in the cold stadium were still on their feet in wild applause. Into the roaring din walked Mathias to accept the embrace of brother Jimmy, sitting in the athletes' bleachers. As he flopped into the arms of the tall eighteen-year-old blond, Bob intoned:

"You take it from here, Jimmy."

Jimmy is a coming decathlon star, and Bob's request sounded as if he were through with sports' most brutal contest.

Flash bulbs exploded as Bob and Jimmy tried to talk. Other athletes and coaches were upon Bob now, pummeling his shoulders and back. Newsmen were next to arrive. As Bob quietly answered their drum-fire of questions, Hamilton commented:

"Who says nice guys don't win?"

Hordes of teen-age girls were converging on Bob from all sections of the stadium. Hurriedly excusing himself, he again broke into a run, this time for the dressing room. As Bob entered, the door was quickly shut—and bolted.

From his dressing room quarters, Bob walked to the window and gazed out at the scoreboard, which emblazoned his 7,887 points.

"That looks pretty good," he told newsmen, "but you watch that Milty Campbell. He's a great athlete and a great guy. He'll probably break that mark at Melbourne."

Bob's conquest, almost a duplication of his triumph

at London, paced a United States sweep in the most important of all the Olympic events. Campbell came in second with 6,989 points, followed by Floyd Simmons with 6,785.

When Bob finished, it was too late for a victory ceremony. Besides, Prof. Martti Parantainen's band, which had played national anthems for the winners, had departed for the night. It would be best, all agreed, to hold the ceremony next day.

In the bowels of the stadium Bob continued to answer the questions of sports writers and Olympic officials.

He was a different athlete from the one who faced many of the same persons after the London Olympics.

"I've had more tiring days," Bob conceded, as he sipped tomato juice. "You generally feel aches and pains all over after running the 1,500 meters, but right now, except for the pain in my leg, I feel perfectly fresh. It's been a wonderful meet. And it will be my last one."

The writers nodded knowingly, for Mathias had said the same thing after his victory at London. He'll be only twenty-five when the Melbourne Olympics roll around—just in his prime.

Had he expected to set a new record? What was the condition of his leg?

"Well, after the high hurdles yesterday," replied Mathias, "I didn't think I could do it. And my leg hurt pretty much today. I also had the feeling today during the pole vault that I couldn't beat the record, but right then I began getting the breaks."

The roar of the crowd for the iron-muscled, iron-willed American still could be heard from the dressing quarters.

Just then a Finnish official entered. He went directly to Mathias.

"Bob," he said, "the crowd refuses to leave. You know the decathlon always excites us Finns. The crowd wants to see you again. Could you, would you oblige?"

"Why, of course," said Mathias.

Like a Greek hero of old, Bob swung around the infield inside the track, where he had just finished the 1,500-meter run. He waved to the throng as he circled back toward the dressing room. The fans let go with a mighty volley of applause which shook the concrete structure. Then, contented, they began to file out.

Before Bob gained the locker room door, he ran into a swarm of bobby-soxers, who had leaped over the rail. Looking as fit and fresh as if he had just dropped in for the competition, he remained until all the girls had their prized signature.

Mathias is as much Tulare's hero as Olympia's and, meantime, things were popping again in the little California town. Tulare's time is nine hours behind Helsinki's, and by 1:30 P.M. just about everyone in town had heard the news.

Sirens shrieked out the glad tidings to the citizens, who yearly seem to grow more enthusiastic over Bob's triumphs. This time they danced and paraded in the streets to the detonations of smoke bombs.

As the news reached an anxiously awaiting crowd at

Hotel Tulare, a parade of hundreds of cars, trucks and even farm vehicles was formed.

Many of the marchers carried placards which hailed not only Mathias but also Sim Iness, Bob's high school teammate, who was a surprise winner of the discus at Helsinki. Thus, tiny Tulare, alone among the cities of the world, produced two Gold Medal winners in men's track at Helsinki. The great metropolises, such as London, New York and Moscow, just weren't in it with the little California town.

Among those who reported early to the Tulare Hotel to await the news was Mrs. C. M. (Lillian) Mathias, the champion's mother. At the hotel a special teletype had been hooked up to feed information to an improvised scoreboard.

"I just couldn't stand to stay home," she explained. Shortly after Dr. Mathias arrived. Although Mrs. Mathias never doubted that Robert would win, she broke down with emotion when the news was received.

"It's simply wonderful," she sobbed. "I just knew he would come through—even if he had to do it on one leg."

After complete results were in, she and her husband, arm-in-arm, walked out into the street to the delirious cheers of their friends. The bright San Joaquin Valley sun, in contrast to the drab skies of Helsinki, smiled down a benediction on the happy scene.

The country doctor turned to his wife and remarked:

"I guess Robert did quite a day's work."

And the early celebration, only the prelude to Bob's and Sim's homecoming a month later, swept on into the warm Tulare night.

Chapter 11

WHAT'S AHEAD?

AFTER LEAVING HELSINKI, BOB MATHIAS WENT ON A TOUR of several European countries, in which he participated in exhibition track meets. His plane landed him back in America on August 24, 1952. That night he took a friend dancing at the Tavern-on-the-Green, in New York City's Central Park, and the next afternoon and evening they spent at Coney Island. Then he flew on to the welcome awaiting him in Tulare and other cities of his home state.

As soon as he could, he left with his family for their cabin in Kings Canyon National Park in the Sierras. He couldn't wait to go trout fishing again in the Kings River. He chopped wood, hiked, cooked out, read, and spent hours watching blue jays steal the food he had set out for the chipmunks and squirrels. In fact, he made it very hard for his family, or even himself, to remember he is a world champion.

Now from the dizzy pinnacle he has scaled in a few short years, Bob Mathias can already look back on a

227

history of excitement, achievement and glory such as few mortals compile in a lifetime.

Twice he has been acclaimed champion in the most severe test of athletic dexterity and staying power yet devised by modern man, the decathlon. His name is known around the world. He has broken bread and rubbed shoulders with the great, not only in the sphere of sport, but in all walks of life. He has captured so many awards that, after the 1952 U.S. national decathlon meet and Olympic tryout, a special trophy room of embossed plywood paneling was added to his Tulare home.

Previously, when some brilliant young men have run out of worlds to conquer, they have, like Alexander the Great of Macedonia, sat down and cried. But Mathias is too even-tempered and level-headed for such emotion. He belittles his accomplishments and he's "still from Tulare." Moreover, through his sound upbringing he has developed a sense of responsibility to match these sober times.

In the fall of 1952, as in 1951, Bob's example provided the Stanford football team with its spiritual cue, and theoretically, because he laid out his sophomore season, he would be eligible for another campaign in 1953. But, as a member of a Marine reserve program, Bob is urgently needed as a leader of troops and he plans to graduate on schedule after the spring quarter of 1953. Then will come a short training course at Quantico, Virginia, and commissioning in the greatest uniform he has ever worn.

Many assume that this will signal the formal end of

Mathias' meteoric athletic career. Bob has said that he will never again compete in a decathlon because "it's too hard to train for." In his final college track season he says he will concentrate on two or three events, mainly the discus and hurdles. And in post-Olympic exhibitions in Europe Bob did just that. In one meet in Zurich, without the handicap of having to compete in a virtual one-man track show, he fled over the 110 meter high hurdles in the astonishing time of 13.8 seconds. That was four-tenths of a second better than he had ever done before and caused some running authorities to doubt the result, as only eight men have equalled or surpassed that mark. However, meet officials produced pictures to prove it, and Mathias declared he was sure he had never done better.

"I felt very good, had an excellent start and was helped by ideal weather conditions and a very fast track," he said. He wanted to emphasize what he could do now in individual events. Previously, Bob would often apologize for his decathlon showing, saying, "It just means you're second best at a lot of things, best at none."

But from past experience other track and field sages discount Mathias' professed retirement as decathlon champion. They point out that he said the same thing after the 1948 Olympics, then changed his mind almost overnight. Before donning Stanford moleskins he also had denied he would ever play college football. It is a young man's privilege to change his mind, and these experts feel that by the time the 1956 Olympics come around, Mathias will respond either to pressure or an inner yearning to attempt the fantastic goal of a third successive world decathlon wreath. After all, they stress, his two-year hitch in the Marines will keep him in excellent trim.

Further, by 1956, there may be a blood incentive for Mathias to essay his iron-man role again. If brother Jimmy, a rising track star who will be tutored at Occidental College by one of America's best coaches, Payton Jordan, can improve sufficiently; and if sister Patricia fulfills her ambition of becoming a top swimmer, the Mathiases could become the only American family ever to place three representatives on the same Olympics team.

Bob is bullish about Jimmy's decathlon prospects. Although the latter, with scant practice, finished only nineteenth in a field of twenty-six in the 1952 national decathlon meet, he is capable of considerable improvement. "Jimmy did better his first week in the pole vault and javelin than I ever did," Bob points out. Even if the younger Mathias never approaches Bob's stature as an all-purpose performer, he could excel at a particular skill, such as the discus or shot.

Outside of sports, Bob is a bit uncertain about what sort of career he will follow—natural enough for a young man entering military service. He has declared that he would like either to coach or to land a public relations job with a sporting goods concern or some other related type of business. Certainly for such a calling he has a natural aptitude; he gets along famously with everyone, likes to meet people and would be the finest type of representative any organization could have.

There is the possibility of his appearing in movies or television. Former decathlon greats like Jim Thorpe and Glenn Morris have either played in, or been the subject of, films. Bob already has been approached by Hollywood agents, but he looks askance at strong man roles. He has made some TV appearances, but his dramatic experience has been confined to public school plays. However, he has picked up the necessary poise and he always has had the clean-cut good looks of a video or screen idol. His gold-flecked brown hair, clear blue eyes, soft spoken voice and gangling, reluctant charm give him an appeal that would be irresistible to femininity of almost any culture.

However, Bob is still happiest when he is surrounded by his wonderful family and hometown friends. The Mathias reputation is so solid in the San Joaquin Valley, and even nationally, that it is not beyond the realm of possibility that the citizens there may draft Bob some day for political office.

Bill Leiser, sports editor of the *San Francisco Chronicle,* has suggested that, in view of Bob's world-wide appeal, he be sent about the globe as an ambassador for lasting peace.

When he has the motivation, Mathias can be as serious as a Supreme Court judge. While away at his first Olympics he made certain that friends back home would wire him the results of a local election on school bonds. He has held school and club offices before, and during his final year at Stanford he plans to run for some student body office. This experience has been a practical outlet for the strong sense of moral responsibility fos-

231

tered in him by his family and religious training. In the future the rash of signs booming Mathias for all sorts of political office, that appeared in Tulare after his decathlon victories, might be brandished again in dead seriousness.

But if he does nothing else, the wholesome example he has set for youth throughout the United States will have earned him a permanent place in America's gallery of heroes. In striving to be like him, no boy will go wrong.

Asked what advice he could give to youngsters who sought to follow in his footsteps, Mathias said: "First, get a good coach early. I was lucky. Virgil Jackson at Tulare was like Dink Templeton of Stanford. He was a wonderful teacher and analyzer of form. He would say, 'Hold your arm this way and it would add a couple of feet to your throw.'

"After that, work hard and live right."

On the far Pacific shores, where the nation itself found fulfillment, it has raised up a paragon, embodying all of the virtues of the ideal American. As one of Mathias' Tulare boosters put it: "No matter who you are, you've got to like him if you've seen him the way we have. If you were a mother or a father, Bob's the kind of guy you'd want for a son; if you were a fellow, you'd want him for a pal; and if you were a girl—well, just look at the guy."

That's Bob Mathias, a real-life champion of champions.

Chapter 12

GREATER THAN THORPE!

AT THE COMPLETION OF THE 1912 OLYMPIC GAMES IN Stockholm, another American, Jim Thorpe, was directed to the victory podium. There King Gustav V of Sweden presented to him a bronze bust in the King's likeness for his decathlon win, and a huge jeweled chalice which symbolized his pentathlon victory.

Shaken with emotion, Gustav touched Jim's shoulder. "You, sir," he said, "are the greatest athlete in the world!"

"Thanks, King," replied Thorpe.

In what was intended as a ringing accolade, the King had been guilty of an understatement, for the big Indian was the greatest all-around athlete the world had seen up to that time.

But is he today? No, say many authorities. Instead they give the honor to Bob Mathias.

Thirty-six years after Thorpe's heroics at Stockholm, Mathias at the London Olympics posted a 5-4 edge over the Stockholm marks of the immortal Indian.

Mathias was superior in the 400 meters, shot put,

discus, pole vault and javelin. The pair turned in identical times of 11.2 in the 100-meter dash.

By 1952, when he still had not cast his first vote, Mathias had Thorpe beaten in nine of the ten events, both in the Helsinki Olympics and at the Tulare tryouts. Here's an event-by-event comparison:

	MATHIAS (1952 Olympics)	THORPE (1912 Olympics)
100-meter dash	10.9	11.2
Broad jump	22-10.80	22-2 5/8
Shot put	50-2.37	42-5 3/8
High jump	6-2.81	6-1 5/8
400-meter run	50.2	52.2
110-meter hurdles	14.7	15.6
Discus	153-10.06	121-3 7/8
Pole vault	13-1.16	10-7 15/16
Javelin	194-3.15	149-11 3/16
1,500 meter run	4:50.8	4:40.1

As the population of the world grows, so grows the competition in sports. And if Thorpe in his prime had competed in the Helsinki decathlon, he would have been whipped, too, by both Milton Campbell and Floyd Simmons, who placed behind Mathias for an American sweep.

Many, including Brutus Hamilton, coach of America's 1952 Olympic track team, rate Bob over Jim on the basis of his track superiority.

Explained Hamilton:

"Since running, jumping and throwing have been the basis of measuring athletic ability since the dawn of history, I think that we can safely consider Bob Mathias the greatest athlete up to our time. And I believe it will be a long time before his equal appears on our earth."

Mathias has won two Olympic decathlons, as compared with Thorpe's one, and Bob could probably make the score three at Melbourne in 1956.

Since 1924, only the decathlon has been offered trackmen, so Mathias has had no chance of matching Thorpe's trick of taking both the decathlon and pentathlon (five events).

The pentathlon of today is entirely apart from track. It consists of such sports as horseback riding and shooting. The pentathlon of Thorpe's day, discontinued after the 1920 Olympics, was a track and field event; in fact, a lesser decathlon.

Like Thorpe, Mathias is a standout in any sport he cares to try, and it was in football and track that both men found fame, though they traveled diverse trails. Thorpe first made headlines as a halfback for the Carlisle Indians and followed by his double Olympic victory at Stockholm.

Conversely, Mathias won world renown first in track. Later, after staying out of football at Stanford for a year, he led the lightly regarded Redshirts to the 1952 Rose Bowl game.

It's not likely that Mathias, miracle man that he is, can ever match Thorpe's grid greatness, for he has no plan for a pro career now. In four blazing seasons at little Carlisle, the wild Indian devastated the top powers of the East. After college he starred with the Canton Bulldogs and he continued to play pro ball until he was forty-two years old.

In baseball Thorpe failed to stick with the New York Giants. Like Mathias, he was a fine basketball player and, moreover, was skilled in wrestling, swimming, lacrosse, tennis and archery.

But Mathias, who has amazing reflexes and coordination, probably would be better than Thorpe at most sports.

Observed Hamilton: "Bob has the rare knack of imitative learning. I'm sure there's no sport he couldn't master in a few weeks."

That's the way it was with golf. After watching his brother Gene, an expert golfer, Bob, while a Stanford sophomore, shot an 81 on his third time out.

During the winter of 1951–52, Mathias made more than one trip with his Fiji friends to Dodge Ridge, a popular nearby ski resort in the Sonora Pass Vacationland. Fortunately, neither his football coach nor his track coach heard about it. Otherwise, there would have been no sleep for either.

Since college baseball conflicts with track, Mathias has had no opportunity as yet to try the national pastime. But Everett Dean, Stanford's baseball coach, claims that Bob still could be a big leaguer if he only had the desire. His judgment is based on Mathias' easy movements.

Bob's only approach to baseball came one summer when he was in high school. Before it was time to head for the YMCA camp, he tried his hand in the Tulare softball league. He was particularly effective with his bat, hitting around the .500 mark, but by the time word of his feats had reached the scouts, he was off to the mountains.

Like Thorpe, Mathias is a skilled swimmer. He

learned to swim in the Junior Red Cross program when he was only six years old. By the time he had reached high school, with many dips in the irrigation canals behind him, Bob was both a crack diver and swimmer, but, because of the conflict with track, he had no chance to represent Tulare High as a swimmer. However, he did set a couple of school swim marks in his gym class.

Probably no other athlete since Red Grange has been so relaxed as Mathias, though at the same time he's a great competitor. Bob can fall asleep anywhere, anytime, in less than ten minutes, and then he sleeps like a log. His Phi Gamma Delta brethren at Stanford have found by test that a horn blown in his face won't wake him. They even applied dye to his locks as he dozed in his chair in the spring of 1952 without disturbing his snooze. Often Bob has fallen asleep in the dressing room before an important athletic event. It seems that sleep comes ahead of everything else in his training program. On the door of his room at Helsinki was this sign: "Do not disturb after 10 P.M."

Mathias would have a strong edge over Thorpe in the matter of conditioning. After conquering the anemia of his boyhood, Bob adhered to a spartan training schedule. He follows a year-round protein-heavy, starch-free diet. Thorpe was less regular in his habits, and it's doubtful that he would have had the endurance for a second Olympic test.

In his entire athletic career, Bob has shown no visible signs of nervousness. Outside it, he's been tied up but once. That was at the marriage January 20, 1951, of brother Eugene to Priscilla Hawkes, of Windham, Me. A formal wedding, it was performed in the Tulare Methodist Church by its pastor, Rev. Douglas Ewan. Just before the rites got under way, Bob, the best man, began cracking his knuckles, twisting his class ring and biting his lips. Sweat broke out on his forehead. Noticing his brother's uneasiness, Gene whispered: "Look, Bob. Rev. Ewan's wearing Stanford's colors for us tonight." A red stole was draped across the minister's white robe as if in salute to the two Stanford students. After this remark Bob laughed, relaxed, and the ceremony proceeded smoothly.

Regulated meals, fresh air, constant exercise and an abundance of sleep have equipped Mathias with a perfect body. In fact, it was noted at the Helsinki Olympics that he was better put together than the Discobolus, a statue by the Greek sculptor Myron, which for centuries has reflected the supposedly ultimate physique for trackmen.

At six feet, three inches, Bob has the long stride of a hurdler. At 199 pounds he is big enough for the weight events. His leg muscles are those of a sprinter, his back muscles resemble a pole vaulter's and his outsized chest stores enough wind for a marathon runner. In short, a perfect specimen.

Though largely overlooked, feet are just about an athlete's most important equipment. And here again Mathias has been liberally endowed.

Conrad Jarvis, Stanford's athletic trainer, holds that Bob has the best constructed pair of feet he's ever examined. They're large—he wears a size 13½ shoe—but that's what gives Mathias his fine sense of balance.

"Bob's feet," said Jarvis, "are both well-formed and well-developed. And there isn't a trace of fungus or athlete's foot. Actually, his pair of feet are one-in-a-million.

"Many athletes have good hands but unfortunate feet. Stress and strain of rigorous athletic competition have a telling effect on the bony network that makes up one's feet. Big men with small bones are continually suffering from the strains of the metatarsal arch, caused by excessive weight. Mathias has large bones in his feet, which show no effect of the pounding to which they've been submitted."

A doctor at Moffett Field who examined Bob when he applied for Marine training said that Mathias easily was the finest physical specimen among the thousands he had seen.

A close student of recent decathlons is impressed more than anything else by Mathias' durability. In every decathlon in which he has competed several men have dropped out, and often it was the better athletes. In Bob's first decathlon—the Southern Pacific AAU—UCLA's Al Lawrence, the favorite, was unable to finish, as well as seven others in the field of thirty-nine. And in Mathias' second test—the 1949 nationals—his foremost rival, Moon Mondschein, fell from the running the second day because of a sore arm. That's the way it was in about every meet, including the 1952 Olympic decathlon, in which France's Ignace Heinrich, expected to press Bob, was forced out by an injured ankle.

The strain was equally telling on Bob but after his injuries he always managed to keep going.

When Virgil Jackson, Mathias' high school coach, was asked what made the kid tick as an athlete, he dissected him thus: 1) his natural ability; 2) his response to the call of competition; 3) his method and manner of living.

Four years later Ray Dean, Stanford's assistant track coach, had this appraisal of the campus hero: "You can't predict what Mathias can do. All you can be sure of is that he will win. He is absolutely the greatest athlete I have ever coached or seen. He is the dream competitor —the one in a million who has the temperament to match the talent."

The Rev. Robert Richards, winner of the pole vault in the Helsinki Olympics, is confident that no other athlete ever approached Mathias for all-around ability. "Just vaulting alone does me in," confessed Richards. "But Bob goes on to nine other events which are just as tough. The decathlon is the supreme athletic test, and no other man has passed it so well."

Shortly after Mathias won his first Olympic title, the argument opened as to whether he is a better all-around athlete than Thorpe. Early asked to express an opinion, Coach Jackson asserted:

"I really don't know which is the better since I never saw Thorpe. But I have seen Bob and, if Thorpe has the edge, at least he wasn't as good as Bob at seventeen. I'd have to see him to believe that he was ever as good as Mathias. I used to think that Jackie Robinson

240

of UCLA was the world's greatest all-around athlete, but that was before I met Bob."

Later Jackson wrote in the *Tulare County School Bulletin*:

> Many college coaches have inquired as to what sort of a boy Bob Mathias is. This is my answer: he is an example for all the youths of America. Here is a boy who trained to perfection. He was a boy with a burning desire to be a great athlete. Bob is the type of boy who will make any sacrifice necessary to keep his God-given ability in perfect working order. He responded to competition. When the chips were down, he came through. Truly there is no more deserving of the title: the greatest athlete in the world!

Former athletes found Mathias' victory at London hard to believe. Among those astounded by the feat was Glen Morris, who had set at the 1936 Olympics a decathlon record which held until 1950, when Bob broke it. Over the telephone from his bedside in an Oakland Hospital in the summer of 1948, Morris told Alan Ward, sports editor of the *Oakland Tribune:*

"I don't see how the boy did it at the age of seventeen and with such short preparation. I concentrated on the decathlon for five years before Berlin, four in college and one after graduation—yet this kid beat several of my marks."

Overlooked by all the experts is the weather factor which makes Mathias' marks so much the more remarkable. Both Morris and Thorpe enjoyed warm dry weather during their Olympic decathlon competition, but Bob was forced to fight both rain and cold at London and Helsinki.

After Mathias had shattered the world decathlon record at Tulare in 1950 with a harvest of 8,042 points (under the old scoring system), Dean Cromwell, who coached America's 1948 Olympic track team, held the performance equal to Babe Ruth's sixty home runs or Bobby Jones' Grand Slam in golf. Other track authorities deemed it the equivalent of the fabled four-minute mile—yet to be run.

Perhaps the man best qualified to answer the question is Glen (Pop) Warner, who coached both Thorpe and another great all-arounder, Ernie Nevers. Since Pop lives in Palo Alto, he has had the opportunity to follow Mathias in his Stanford career.

Declared Warner, after much prodding: "Mathias is the closest thing to a miracle athlete I've seen in sixty years."

Dan Ferris, national AAU secretary-treasurer, who saw Thorpe's performance at Stockholm, stated: "Of course, you'd have to call Mathias the better all-around trackman. Records don't lie. But, with modern training, Thorpe probably would have been as good. And, when it comes to other sports, you probably must give the old Indian the edge."

Like the argument as to whether Jack Dempsey in his prime could have whipped Joe Louis in his, the Mathias-Thorpe controversy never will end—unless Bob should change his mind about professional football after his Marine service and make a huge success in it.

242

GREATER THAN THORPE!

How does Mathias himself compare football with the decathlon? Which is the tougher?

"There's no comparison," said Bob. "Football just isn't in it with the decathlon."

But suppose there was no platoon system in football and you had to play every minute on both offense and defense. Would you still say the decathlon is tougher?

"Absolutely," affirmed the Stanford star.

With characteristic modesty, Mathias is not so sure that he even rates as a better trackman than Thorpe. "If Mr. Thorpe had had the same fine coaching, equipment and competition that I and other athletes of to-day have," said Bob, "I'd sure hesitate to say that I could beat him if we met in our prime."

Incidentally, the two men met but once—at the *Los Angeles Times'* Sports Award dinner in 1948.

If the matter were left to a world-wide vote, Mathias, of course, would win in a landslide, for football is not known outside the United States. Neither to any great extent is baseball—the other sport in which Thorpe surpasses Mathias at this time.

Certainly Mathias would take almost all the votes of Greater London, the world's largest city, which saw him whip the earth's best, as well as all the votes of the little American town of Tulare.

And sentiment is about the same over the rest of the world, where, as Hamilton pointed out, track and field —or athletics—has been the standard of measuring athletic prowess since the dawn of history.

APPENDIX

Bob Mathias' U.S. and Olympic Decathlon Record

	1. *June 10-11, 1948*	2. *June 25-26, 1948*
		Combined
	"Pasadena Games"	National AAU Decathlon
	Pacific AAU Decathlon	Olympic Tryouts
	Memorial Coliseum	Foley Field
Event	Los Angeles	Bloomfield, N. J.
100 meters	11.3 sec.	11.2 sec.
Broad jump	21' 4 1/2"	21' 6 5/8"
Shot put	43' 1"	42' 6 5/8"
High jump	5' 10"	6'
400-meter run	52.1 sec.	51 sec.
110-meter hurdles	15.7 sec.	15.1 sec.
Discus	140' 1/8"	139' 7 1/4"
Pole vault	11' 9"	11' 6"
Javelin	175' 4 5/8"	157' 3 3/8"
1,500 meters	4:59.2	4:55.2
Total:	7,094 points	7,224 points

Event	3. Aug. 5-6, 1948 XIV Olympics Empire Stadium Wembley, London England	4. June 28-29, 1949 National AAU Decathlon Tulare High Stadium
100 meters	11.2 sec.	11.3 sec.
Broad jump	21' 8 1/3"	22' 4 1/2"
Shot put	42' 9 1/4"	45' 3"
High jump	6' 1 1/4"	6' 1/4"
400-meter run	51.7 sec.	51.3 sec.
110-meter hurdles	15.7 sec.	15 sec.
Discus	144' 4"	150' 11 1/8"
Pole vault	11' 5 3/4"	11' 6"
Javelin	165' 1"	177' 10 7/8"
1,500 meters	5:11	4:58.2
Total:	7,139 points	7,556 points

Event	5. June 27-28, 1950 National AAU Decathlon Tulare High Stadium	6. July 2-3, 1952 National Decathlon Tulare High Stadium
100 meters	10.9 sec.	10.8 sec.
Broad jump	23' 3 3/8"	23' 5 1/4"
Shot put	47' 6 1/4"	49' 10 7/8"
High jump	6' 3/4"	6' 2 3/4"
400-meter run	51 sec.	50.8 sec.
110-meter hurdles	14.7 sec.	14.6 sec.
Discus	146' 5"	157' 11 5/8"
Pole vault	13' 3/4"	12' 3 3/4"
Javelin	182' 4 1/2"	193' 10 3/8"
1,500 meters	5:05	4:55.3
Total:	8,042 points	7,825 points *

7. July 25-26, 1952

XV OLYMPICS
HELSINKI
FINLAND

EVENT	
100 meters	10.9 sec.
Broad jump	22' 10.80"
Shot put	50' 2.37"
High jump	6' 2.81"
400-meter run	50.2 sec.
110-meter hurdles	14.7 sec.
Discus	153' 10.06"
Pole vault	13' 1.16"
Javelin	194' 3.15"
1,500 meters	4:50.8

Total: 7,887 points *

1949 Oslo, Norway exhibition 7,346 points.
1950 Switzerland exhibition 7,312 points.
1950 Exhibition at Stanford 7,602 points.

* New point system. A further revision of the decathlon scoring system in process of compilation, will raise the 1952 total to 8,125 points.